Mrs. Thomas F. Bayard
with respectful regards
Daniel Ravenel
Charles S. Vedder.

April 13 1890
Charleston S.C.

THE LITURGY,

OR

FORMS OF DIVINE SERVICE,

OF

The French Protestant Church,

OF

CHARLESTON, S. C.

TRANSLATED FROM THE LITURGY OF THE CHURCHES OF NEUFCHATEL AND VALLANGIN:

EDITIONS OF 1737 AND 1772.

WITH SOME ADDITIONAL PRAYERS,

CAREFULLY SELECTED.

THE WHOLE ADAPTED TO PUBLIC WORSHIP IN THE UNITED STATES OF AMERICA.

THIRD EDITION.

NEW YORK:
ANSON D. F. RANDOLPH & COMPANY,
770 BROADWAY, COR. 9TH STREET.

EDWARD O. JENKINS,
PRINTER AND STEREOTYPER,
NO. 20 N. WILLIAM ST., N. Y.

TABLE OF CONTENTS.

PART FOURTH.

PREFACE

TO THE FIRST EDITION,

PUBLISHED IN 1713.

THE Churches in the Principality of Neufchatel and Vallangin began some years since to establish the Liturgy, which is now presented to the public. In order that it might appear in a better state, it was deemed advisable that some time should elapse before its publication. The resolution has at length been taken to print it, in conformity with the wish of many, who have desired that it should be made public.

It is not necessary here to enlarge on the utility and antiquity of Liturgies, or to explain how important it is that the mode of celebrating divine service should be well regulated. None can doubt that St. Paul's maxim, "Let all things be done decently and in order," * is applicable to the worship of God in the religious assemblies of Christians. This worship is of the greatest consequence in religion, because it consists chiefly in serving God, in adoring him, in giving him thanks, and in calling upon him. Hence it is indispensable that divine service should be so performed as to be most worthy of that infinite Being, and best adapted to raise men to him, and to fill them with reverence and love for his Supreme Majesty.

The attainment, however, of this end is difficult, unless there be an established form of public worship. When the order of divine service is settled, it is celebrated as well by the Minister as by the People, in a manner more edifying, grave and decorous,

* 1 Epis. Cor., ch. xiv., v. 40.

than when it is entrusted to the discretion of the Clergy. The preservation of uniformity in worship is another valuable consequence of Liturgies. And if they conform to the spirit of the Gospel, they exert also a salutary influence, in excluding from the Church practices and opinions inconsistent with the purity of religion.

These, and some other considerations, have satisfied the Pastors of the Churches of Neufchatel and of Vallangin, that they should contribute to the edification of *their flocks*, by settling the forms and order of their Liturgy, and by imitating, in this particular, the example of most Protestant Churches, and especially of the Churches of Switzerland, whose Liturgies are all printed.

That which is here given to the public contains, *first*, the form of divine service for Sundays and for week days, when a sermon is preached; afterwards the prayers for divers occasions, whether before or after the sermon; in the third place, the manner of celebrating divine service, morning and afternoon, when there is no preaching; in the last place, the formularies for the celebration of the sacraments, for the solemnization of matrimony, for the admission of catechumens, and for the reconciliation of penitents.*

To set forth here all the reflections which might be made on the different parts of this Liturgy is unnecessary. It has been judged advisable, however, to say something on the objects proposed, and on the method which has been followed in its composition.

This Liturgy has been formed, as far as practicable, from the Scriptures, and from ancient and modern Liturgies. The Scriptures, especially, have been consulted—for as they are the sole rule of our faith, so are they the only perfect guide to the true mode of serving God. This course has been chiefly pursued in the Canticles for the ordinary Morning and Afternoon Service. They have been drawn, almost word for word, from the sacred volume, and especial care hath been taken that they should em-

* When this Liturgy was first published, certain scandalous sinners, who had been excluded from the Church, were received again into its peace: but this practice hath been abolished, for reasons which it is useless to mention, and the formulary only serves for individuals, at the meeting of the Consistory, where it has been preserved.

brace those excellent passages of the New Testament which relate to Jesus Christ and our redemption. This has been thought the more necessary, because hitherto our Churches have not had, like other Protestant Churches, any Christian Canticles, and we have therefore sung only those of the book of Psalms.* It is, moreover, undeniable, that if the Jews praised God for the favours which he had granted to their nation, and if they showed forth his benefits in their songs, Christians are under still higher obligations to bless God, through Jesus Christ; to celebrate the holy name of their Redeemer, to sing his praises, and to speak in their hymns of all that he hath done for them, of his coming into the world, of his sufferings, of his resurrection, of his ascension, of his last and glorious advent, and of the salvation which he hath purchased for them. † The Apostles do expressly command Christians to praise God our Father, through Jesus Christ his Son, and their writings abound with praises and thanksgivings, which ought to be without ceasing in the mouths and hearts of the faithful. Authors who wrote in the second century, and on whom we may rely, ‡ inform us that the first Christians in their assemblies sang hymns to Jesus Christ as to a God, and that, in the celebration of the Eucharist, God, the father of all things, was praised and glorified, through the Son and Holy Spirit. Much more might be said upon this subject, but the reader is referred to the preface, which is at the head of the Christian Canticles, lately introduced by the Church of Geneva into their worship. In the Canticles of this Liturgy are collected the principal passages of the New Testament, which can be embodied in the worship of Christians; and they have been interspersed among those of the Old. These passages being very numerous, several Canticles have been composed, as well for the ordinary service as for particular occasions.

After the Scriptures, the best Liturgies, both ancient and modern, have been consulted. Several formularies, previously adop-

* Since the first edition of this work, several Canticles, written by different authors, have become a part of public worship, and are sung on the principal solemnities, instead of the Psalms of David, which are reserved for ordinary occasions.

† Ep. Eph. i., 3 and v. 19; Coloss. iii. 16; I. Pet. i., 3; Apoc. i., 6, etc.

‡ Pliny the younger, in his letter to the Emperor Trajan (Epistle 97). Justin Martyr, in his first Apology.

ted in the Churches of this country, have been retained, and in many respects a conformity has been observed to the order already established therein; and from other Liturgies, especially the ancient, whatever appeared the most edifying has been selected. In matters of worship, the practice of the past ages of the Church is entitled to great consideration: and it must be confessed that in the prayers of the Primitive Christians, their spirituality and simplicity are very remarkable. Besides, who can doubt that whatever was done in those days, and had been established by the successors of the Apostles, did conform to the spirit of the Gospel, and ought to command the respect of all Christians. The customs of the Churches did indeed afterwards vary exceedingly. Primitive simplicity was departed from, and Liturgies were burthened with many things, not merely useless, but even contrary to the purity of evangelical worship. This remark is applicable to such as have descended to us. It is, however, certain that the foundation and the essence of the ancient worship have been preserved in almost all Liturgies. If, therefore, whatever is peculiar to each Liturgy, and whatever was added from time to time, as ignorance, error, and superstition prevailed in the Church, be laid aside, and only so much be retained, as ancient general usage sanctioned and all Liturgies agree in, we shall undoubtedly have the genuine form of primitive Christian worship. Such a proceeding would be also one of the best methods for the attainment of that uniformity, which is so desirable for the peace and edification of the Church.

We have aimed in this Liturgy at the utmost simplicity and perspicuity. So far from seeking, we have avoided the ornaments of language, affected emphasis in terms, preambles, periods over long, reasonings too extended, and figurative expressions, such excepted as, being taken from the Scriptures, are clear to the readers of the sacred writings. We have endeavored to express, in the most simple and natural manner, the sentiments and emotions with which we ought to be filled in the presence of God. The language of devotion is the language of the heart; it is artless and affecting. The reverence due to the Divine Majesty, and the edification of the people, require this simplicity; and the Holy Scriptures teach us thus to pray. The prayers and the praises found in the Sacred Books, especially in the Psalms, are only the emotions of the heart, which for the most part have little connection. In the Lord's Prayer, that great model of Christian supplication, we also find extreme simplicity, with singular brevity.

This brevity also has been the subject of very particular attention. When Liturgies are too long, and the service is unreasonably extended, public worship is less frequented, and its very length may diminish attention and devotion. We have anxiously endeavored to avoid this, especially in the service for the week-days. It is certain that religious exercises ought not to last long on such days; because they are days of business. Hence the ordinary service for these days has been so regulated as not to extend beyond twenty minutes, and at the utmost, though rarely, not beyond half an hour.

We have also judged it right to vary the formularies of prayer and praise; and to compose some for particular occasions. This diversity serves to awaken attention, which is more easily relaxed, when the same things are continually heard. It is moreover peculiarly proper to direct and animate the devotion of the people on the most solemn occasions; nothing being more reasonable than that our prayers should be adapted to the seasons and circumstances, in which we are actually placed.

In the last place, this Liturgy is not so fixed, nor are we so restricted in it, that some changes may not be made either by retrenching or adding, as circumstances may require; as when we are called to return thanks to God for some particular benefit, or to avert his wrath in seasons of calamity.

After these general reflections, it is deemed expedient to add some respecting the third part of this Liturgy, which comprises the ordinary service for Morning and the Afternoon.

It has been our object to embrace in this service all the acts of divine worship. These are to confess our sins, to adore God, to praise him, to render him thanks, to consecrate ourselves to him, to call upon him, and to read his word. All these acts, to wit, confession, adoration, praise, self-dedication, and invocation, have not been comprehended in a single prayer; but are set forth separately and distinctly, that all, even the most simple, may understand what they are doing, whilst engaged in public worship; that they may comprehend in what this worship consists, and that they may be able to distinguish its several parts. For the same reason, there is an interval between each prayer, and the word Amen closes each. These intervals serve to direct and fix the devotion of the people. Each person may, during those moments, recollect himself, and lift up his heart to God, either to thank him for some favour, or to ask some particular grace. They serve also to recall the absent, and to awaken attention, which would easily wander during a long prayer, in which all the acts of religious worship should be expressed in uninterrupted succession. But they would be more profitable, if the people would answer Amen, at the end of each part of the service; a practice observed in the days of the Apostles, and of which we have incontestable proofs in the 14th chapter of 1st Epistle to the Corinthians, wherein St. Paul, speaking of praying in an unknown tongue, says, "when thou shalt bless with the spirit, how shall he that occupieth the room of the unlearned say Amen, at thy giving of thanks?" This custom of replying Amen is very ancient. God had commanded the people of Israel to answer Amen to the maledictions, which were to be pronounced at the top of Mount Ebal.* It appears from the 16th chapter of Chron. B. 1st, † and from the end of the 106th Psalm, and that the people replied Amen, in the intervals of prayer and praise: for we there read these words, "Blessed be the Lord God of Israel, from everlasting to everlasting, and let all the people say Amen." The same thing is seen in the 8th chapter of Nehemiah, v. 6. "And Ezra blessed the Lord, the great God, and all the people answered Amen, Amen, lifting up their hands." This was wisely ordered: this Amen signified that all the congregation assented to what was said in the prayers and Canticles. In truth, the people ought not to attend on divine service merely as auditors and spectators, nor ought they merely to follow in thought that which is uttered by the ministers of the church; but they also ought to speak on their part, and at least to answer Amen to all that is spoken in the name of the assembly. It is admitted that the ancient mode of celebrating service was by parts or intervals, and by antiphones, that is to say, responses. We find this by the words of the 147th Psalm: "Sing to the Lord, answering one to the other." In this manner were recited several Psalms of praise, as the 118th, 134th, and the 136th. The primitive Christians retained this practice in their

* Deut. ch. xxvii. v. 15–26. † 1 Chron. ch. xvi. v. 36—Ps. cvi. v. 48.

worship, and especially in that excellent and admirable Liturgy, which they employed for the communion service. The ministers * and the deacons said to the people, "Lift up your hearts on high," the people answered, "Our hearts are lifted up unto the Lord." The ministers added, "Let us return thanks to the Lord our God," the people replied, "It is just and reasonable that we should return him thanks." And all the communicants answered Amen † to the prayers and thanksgivings of the ministers. Moreover, the above expressions, which are in the ancient Liturgies of the Holy Supper, and of which they form a chief part, are so beautiful and edifying, and correspond so well to that sacred ceremony, that we have believed it right to adopt them into the Liturgy prepared for the Churches of this country. The other parts of this Liturgy have been taken from those which are used in different Protestant Churches.

But one of the principal objects contemplated in the form of worship for the ordinary Morning and Evening service, was to re-establish the reading of the Scriptures, as a part of public worship. To set forth all the forcible and urgent reasons, which show that we are under an absolute necessity to have the Bible read in the assemblies of the Church would be superfluous. This has always formed an essential part of divine service,‡ both among Jews and Christians. The Jews read the sacred books, at their solemn feasts, and in their synagogues. They had even divided the books of Moses into as many sections as there are Saturdays in the year, in order that these books might be read entirely through, once in every year, on the Sabbath days. § When the reading was finished, a doctor, or some other person designated, delivered a discourse on what had been read. We see in the eighth chapter of Nehemiah, that this was practised after the return from the captivity. The Levites, says the sacred author, read in the Book of the Law of God distinctly, and gave the sense and caused them to understand the reading. St. Luke relates, ‖ that our Lord having entered the Synagogue of Nazareth, on the Sabbath day, read the sixty-

* St. Cyril of Jerusalem, in his 5th Mystological Catechism.

† Justin Martyr in his first Apology.

‡ Deut. ch. xxxi. v. 9, 10, 11.—Nehem. ch. viii. v. 9.

§ See the Acts of the Apostles, chap. xiii. 27.

‖ St. Luke, chap. iv.

first chapter of Isaiah, and then spoke to the persons present, showing that the words which he had just read were fulfilled in his own person.

We again read in the thirteenth chapter of the book of Acts, * that St. Paul and St. Barnabas went into the Synagogue of Antioch on the Sabbath day, and after the reading of the Law and the Prophets, the Rulers of the Synagogue sent to them, saying, "Men and Brethren, if ye have any word of exhortation for the people, say on." The Christian Church conformed to this practice, and regulated its discipline and worship in this as in various other particulars, by the usages in the assemblies of the Jews. The first Christians read the Scriptures in their assemblies; and so regularly was this done, that in those times one would have thought divine service had not been performed, if the Scriptures had not been read. When the chapter was finished, the head of the assembly gave a brief explanation of it, and exhorted those present, according to the circumstances and wants of the Church. A very ancient author, and one worthy of credit,† who wrote in the second century, thus relates the usage in his time in Christian assemblies. On the Lord's day we assembled together, and the writings of the Apostles and Prophets were read as long as the time would permit. When the reading was finished, he who presided delivered a discourse to instruct the people, and exhort them to the observance of the excellent things which they had heard. This being done, we all rose up and presented our prayers to God. Tertullian who lived a little after the martyr Justin says ‡ that the first Christians assembled to read the sacred books and to exhort the people. However, these exhortations were not always made, and even at that time all the ministers of the church did not preach; but they never failed to read some portion of the Scriptures, and when the reading and the exhortation were over, they resumed the worship, and concluded the service with prayer.

Such was formerly the mode of worship, and such the origin of sermons. The sermons were at first only an interruption of worship and an addition to the reading, and were not regarded, as by many at the present day, the most important part of public

* Acts, chap. xiii. 14, 15. † The martyr Justin, in his First Defence. ‡ In his Apology, 24, 39.

service, and the principal object for which the people assembled. The preaching is, without doubt, very useful, provided it be done with clearness and simplicity; but it is quite necessary that the Scriptures should be read in the church, and in such a manner, that the people may understand that this reading is an essential part of worship.

Nor does it suffice that they be read in the churches before the assembly is formed, or the worship commences. Such reading does not constitute a part of divine service. It is distinguished from it by the time, by the persons who read, and by other circumstances, so that the people pay little attention and respect to it, and the greater part of them are not present, which circumstance proves that they regard the reading of the Holy Scriptures as less important than the preaching. It is for these reasons that the leaders of the churches thought themselves indispensably obliged to re-establish the reading of the word of God in their worship. And as circumstances for a long time had not permitted them to introduce this reading in all the services, and particularly in that of Sunday, they have done it at least in the ordinary morning and evening services. This reading is performed in the following manner:

The Old and New Testaments are read alternately; and the lessons have been so arranged, that the historical books of the Old Testament, from Genesis to Esther, are read in the same time with all the books of the New Testament. After which the New Testament is recommenced with the book of Job, and finished with Malachi.

Thus we read the New Testament twice whilst we read the Old but once. Some chapters and passages are omitted, as the first book of Chronicles, the first chapter of Numbers, and some others. We do not read consecutively, the books of Kings and those of Chronicles, because they contain the same histories, but those chapters are selected in which the history is related with the greatest clearness; and for this purpose a kind of harmony has been prepared. When the chapters are very long, or when they contain a great deal of matter, they are divided so as not to overcharge the memories of the hearers, nor extend the service to an inconvenient length. During the festivals, and also at seasons for celebrating the Holy Supper, and in some other circumstances, the portions of Scripture most appropriate to the occasion are read, forming two lessons, formerly called the Epistle and Gospel; and in this they conformed as nearly as possible to the ancient usage of the church, which long since made a wise and judicious selection of the passages of Scripture proper to be read at the principal solemnities of Christians. At the end of this preface will be found the table of lessons for special occasions. In order that the lessons might have more effect, the chapter is preceded by an argument or summary of its contents, of its parts and its object, with the mode of clearing up the general difficulties if there be any. After the chapter some reflections are added in the form of exhortations, in order that the people may depart the more deeply impressed with the things which they have heard. These reflections extend ordinarily to five or six sentences only. These arguments and reflections have been prepared and are read. It has been found expedient to pursue this course, because if left to the discretion of the ministers, many might lose sight of the brevity, simplicity and precision which are requisite in reflections of this kind. Finally, there being in this Liturgy some passages of which persons unacquainted with the customs of our church will not understand the reason, it is proper to say something in explanation of them, especially as many persons abroad have requested information on the subject. The following then, are the observances in our churches, particularly in the town of Neufchatel, where the public exercises of religion are more frequent than in the country.

There is a sermon every Sunday morning, and at mid-day the Catechism; at Neufchatel there is a sermon again in the evening. In the week they preach on Wednesday and Friday morning. On the other days they perform in the forenoon the ordinary morning service, and every day at three o'clock, the afternoon service. These services are performed by the ministers of the church. The people are seated during the reading of the Holy Scriptures, and during the rest of the service they stand up. On Saturday morning, after the close of the service, the pastors, each in his turn, catechise the children of the age of ten years and upwards, until they have communed. They celebrate the Holy Supper of the Lord at four periods in the year, and at each of these, three times, in order that they who may not have been able to partake of the Holy Sacrament at the first celebration, may partake on the following day; and that persons desiring to commune more than once should have the opportunity to do so. The Holy Supper is celebrated 1st at Easter, to wit: on Palm Sunday, Good Friday and Easter day. 2ndly, at Pentecost: on Pentecost Sunday, the following Friday, and Trinity Sunday. 3dly, about the beginning of the month of September, to wit: on the last Sunday of August, the Friday following, and the first Sunday of September. 4thly, at Christmas, to wit: on the two last Sundays of the year, and on Christmas day, and if Christmas fall on Sunday, on the preceding Friday. The reason is thus seen why our Liturgy contains prayers for two communion Sundays at each of these four festivals; why there are prayers to be introduced into the service during two weeks at these seasons, and why in the table of proper lessons, lessons are appointed for the first and second week. The first week is that which precedes the first Sunday for the communion at the Holy Supper, and the second is that which follows it. During these two weeks, general catechetical instruction is given on every Tuesday, Wednesday and Friday after twelve o'clock, and on these catechisms the catechumens who present themselves to be received for the confirmation of the baptismal vow, and for the participation of the Eucharist, are publicly examined. On the Saturday evenings before the celebration of the Lord's Supper, there is a sermon of preparation, with prayers. The same course is observed on the eve of public fast days.

Such are the principal matters which it seemed proper to notice in explanation of this Liturgy. God grant that it may contribute to the advancement of his glory, and of true piety; and that all who use it, may apply it to its true purpose, the worship of God, in spirit and in truth.—AMEN.

A TABLE OF LESSONS

FOR SPECIAL OCCASIONS.

FOR THE NATIVITY.

FIRST WEEK.	FIRST LESSON.	SECOND LESSON.
Monday Morning,	Isaiah XL. 1–11.	St. Luke I. 1–25.
Monday Evening,	Isaiah XL. 1–10 & XII.	St. Luke I. 26–56.
Tuesday Evening,	Isaiah XLIX. 1–23.	St. Luke I. 57–80.
Wednesday Evening,	Malachi III.	St. Matthew XI.
Thursday Morning,	Malachi IV.	St. Matthew III.
Thursday Evening,	Isaiah XLII. 1–12.	St. Luke III. 1–18.
Friday Evening,	Isaiah LII.	St. John I. 1–18.
Saturday Morning,	Hebrews II.	St. John I. 19–51.

SECOND WEEK.	FIRST LESSON.	SECOND LESSON.
Eve of the Nativity,	Isaiah LXII.	St. Matthew I.
Day of the Nativity,	Hebrews I.	St. Luke II. 1–20.
Day after Nativity,	Isaiah IX. 1–6.	St. Luke II. 11–39.

On the other days the following Lessons are read; and they are arranged according to the day upon which the Nativity falls. The Prophecies of the Old Testament are read, which point out the principal circumstances of the advent of Jesus Christ:

Genesis iii. 15, and xlix. 10; Micah v. 2; Isaiah vii. 14, and ix. 5; Daniel ix. 24–27; Haggai ii. 9; and Malachi iv. 1, 5, 6.

These are all read at one time; and the following from the New Testament are added:—

1st Epistle of St. Peter 1. 10–13; Acts xiii. 16–41; 1st Epistle of St. John I: Epistle to Titus ii. 11–15, and iii. 3–7; St. Matthew ii.; St. Luke ii. 40–52; 1st Corinthians xi. 20–32.

FOR THE EVENING OF THE LAST DAY OF THE YEAR.

FIRST LESSON.	SECOND LESSON.
Psalm xxxix. 9–14.	St. Matthew xxiv. 42–51

FOR THE EVENING OF THE FIRST DAY OF THE YEAR.

FIRST LESSON.	SECOND LESSON.
1st Thess. v. 1-11.	St. Matthew xxv. 1-30.

FOR THE PASSOVER.

FIRST WEEK.	FIRST LESSON.	SECOND LESSON.
Monday Morning,	Exodus XII. 1-28.	St. John XI. 47-57; XII. 1-11.
Monday Evening,	Exodus XII. 29-51.	St. John XII. 12-50.
Tuesday Evening,	Exodus XIII. 1-16.	St. John XIII.
Wednesday Evening,	Isaiah LIII.	St. John XIV.
Thursday Morning,	Isaiah LIV.	St. John XV.
Thursday Evening,	Isaiah LV.	St. John XVI.
Friday Morning,	Genesis XXII. 1-19.	St. John XVII.
Saturday Morning,	1st. Peter III. 18-22.	St. Matt. XXI. 1-17.

HOLY WEEK.	FIRST LESSON.	SECOND LESSON.
Monday Morning,	Philip. II. 5-13.	During this week the second Lesson is taken from the four Evangelists, put in harmony. This history is divided into eight readings, so that the particulars of the crucifixion, and the Death of our Lord, are read on Good Friday, and the history of his Burial on Saturday.
Monday Evening,	Isaiah L. 5-10.	
Tuesday Evening,	Isaiah LXII. 11, 12; & LXIII. 1-9.	
Wednesday Evening,	Daniel IX. 20-27.	
Thursday Morning,	Hebrews IX.	
Thursday Evening,	1st Cor. XI. 20-32.	
Good Friday,	Hebrews X. 1-25.	
Saturday Morning,	Romans VI. 1-14.	

FOR EASTER.

	FIRST LESSON.	SECOND LESSON.
Monday Morning,	Colossians III. 1-17.	The history of the Resurrection, taken from the four Evangelists, and put in harmony.
Monday Evening,	1st Cor. XV. 1-34.	
Tuesday Evening,	1st Cor. XV. 35-58.	

FOR THE ASCENSION.

	FIRST LESSON.	SECOND LESSON.
Eve of the Ascension,	2nd Kings II. 1-14.	St. John XIV. 1-19.
Day of the Ascension,	Ephesians IV. 7-16.	The history of the Ascension, from the Evangelist, and from the Acts.
Day after Ascension,	Hebrews X. 11-31.	St. John XVI. 16-33.

FOR PENTECOST.

FIRST WEEK.	FIRST LESSON.	SECOND LESSON.
Wednesday Evening,	Ezekiel XXXVI. 22-28.	St. John III. 1-21.
Thursday Morning,	Hebrews VIII.	St. John V. 19-36.
Thursday Evening,	Isaiah LXI.	St. Luke I. 16-30.
Friday Evening,	Isaiah LV.	St. John VII. 37-43.
Saturday Morning,	Joel II. 28-32.	St. John XIV. 1-17.

SECOND WEEK.	FIRST LESSON.	SECOND LESSON.
Monday Morning,	Acts II.	St. John XIV. 18-31.
Monday Evening,	Acts X.	St. John XV.
Tuesday Evening,	Acts XI. 1-18.	St. John XVI. 1-15.
Wednesday Evening,	1st Cor. XII.	St. John XVI. 16-33.
Thursday Morning,	1st Cor. XIII.	St. John XVII.
Thursday Evening,	1st Cor. XI. 20-32.	St. John XVIII.
Friday Evening,	Romans VIII.	St. John XIX.
Saturday Morning,	Gal. V. 16-26.	St. Matthew XII. 22-45.

FOR THE FIRST MONDAY AFTER TRINITY SUNDAY.

	FIRST LESSON.	SECOND LESSON.
Morning,	Hebrews II.	St. Matt. XXV. 14-30.
Evening,	Eph. IV. 1-16.	St. Matt. XIII. 24-52.

FOR THE HOLY DAYS OF SEPTEMBER.

FIRST WEEK.	FIRST LESSON.	SECOND LESSON.
Friday Evening,	Isaiah LV.	St. John VI. 26-40.
Saturday Morning,	Prov. IX. 1-11.	St. John VI. 41-63.

SECOND WEEK.	FIRST LESSON.	SECOND LESSON.
Monday Morning,	Romans V.	St. Matthew V. 1-20.
Monday Evening,	Colossians I.	St. Matthew V. 21-48.

SECOND WEEK.	FIRST LESSON.	SECOND LESSON.
Tuesday Evening,	1st Peter I.	St. Matthew VI.
Wednesday Evening,	1st Peter II.	St. Matthew VII.
Thursday Morning,	1st Cor. V. 1–22.	St. Luke XIV. 15–24.
Thursday Evening,	1st Cor. XI. 20–32.	St. Matt. XXV. 1–13.
Friday Evening,	1st John III.	St. John XIX.
Saturday Morning,	Gal. V. 13–26.	St. Matt. XXII. 1–14.

FOR THE WEEK OF PUBLIC FASTING.

	FIRST LESSON.	SECOND LESSON.
Monday Morning,	Isaiah I.	St. Matthew III. 1–12.
Monday Evening,	Jeremiah VII.	St. Matt. XXI. 28–44.
Tuesday Evening,	Zacariah VII.	St. Luke XV.
Morning before Fast,	Isaiah LVIII.	St. Matthew VI. 1–18.
Evening after Fast,	Heb. III. 7–19; IV. 1–11.	St. Luke XIII. 1–9.

GENERAL DIRECTIONS.

Any of the Services of this book may begin with a Canticle, Psalm or Hymn, during which the minister and people stand.

In any other part of the services they stand during a Canticle, and sit during a Psalm or Hymn.

The Canticles may be read or chanted.

Part of a Canticle, Psalm or Hymn, may be used instead of the whole.

At the end of the several Prayers the people answer Amen.

In the morning service, besides the Ten Commandments from Exodus xx. 1-17, with the summary of the Law from St. Matthew xxii. 37-40, there shall be two lessons of Scripture. The first shall be taken from any part of the Old Testament, from Genesis to Esther inclusive, being the Historical Books; or from the Prophetical Books of the Old Testaments. The second Lesson shall be taken from the Gospels or Acts of the Apostles, being the Historical Books of the New Testament. In the afternoon service the first Lesson shall be taken out of the Preceptive Books of the Old Testament, from Job to Ecclesiastes; and the second Lesson out of the Epistles, or the Apocalypse, in the New Testament.

On Holy Days the Lessons may be those in the Table.

During the reading of the Ten Commandments and the summary of the Law, the minister and people stand. During the reading of the other lessons of Scripture, the minister stands and the people sit.

On Holy days, and other special occasions of public worship occurring on week-days, the services for the Lord's Day may be used instead of any of the other services, in the discretion of the minister.

PART FIRST.

Morning Service for the Lord's Day.

The Service may commence with one of the following Canticles, unless another Canticle, or a Psalm or Hymn, be specially announced; during which the Minister and People stand.

CANTICLES.

O COME, let us sing unto the Lord; let us heartily rejoice in the Rock of our salvation.

Let us come before his presence with thanksgiving; and show ourselves glad in him with psalms.

O come, let us worship and bow down; let us kneel before the Lord our Maker.

For he is the Lord our God, and we are the people of his pasture, and the sheep of his hand.

Manifold, O God! are thy wondrous and bounteous works: they are more than can be numbered.

In thee we live, and move, and have our being. The testimonies of thy loving-kindness are ever about us.

Thou hast sent thine only Son into the world, to be a propitiation for our sins.

For all these things we bless thee, and we magnify thy glorious name; saying, with the angels and all the heavenly host,

Holy, Holy, Holy, Lord God of hosts! Heaven and earth are full of thy glory, O God, most high.

Let our mouths show forth thy praise for ever.

Let all that hath breath, bless thee for ever and ever.

Glory be to the Father, and to the Son, and to the Holy Ghost; as it was in the beginning, is now, and ever shall be, world without end. *Amen.*

Or this.

COME, and let us present ourselves before the Lord; let us adore him in his temple; let us humble ourselves in his sanctuary.

The Lord is here. How venerable, how sacred is this place! this is the house of God; this is the gate of heaven.

O Lord! God of our fathers, thou art blessed for ever. To thee belong greatness, power, glory, eternity, majesty.

All that is in heaven and in earth is thine; the kingdom is thine.

Thou art a Prince above all things: thou art Sovereign over all. Riches and honour, power and might, are in thy hand.

Now, therefore, O our God! we magnify thee and praise thy glorious name.

Who are we, and who are this people, that we are enabled freely to offer unto thee this service, and this praise?

We are strangers before thee, and our days pass away as a shadow.

Although we are but dust and ashes, behold, we take upon ourselves to speak unto thee.

Let the words of our mouths be acceptable unto thee, O Lord!

Let thy mercy be upon us, O God! as our trust is in thee.

Glory be, etc.

Then the Minister shall say,

OUR help is in the name of the Lord, who made heaven and earth.—*Psalm, cxxiv.*, 8.

Here, and at the end of the several prayers, the People answer

AMEN.

Then the Minister shall say,

Let us pray.

O ALMIGHTY God and heavenly Father! we have come together for the public sanctification of this Lord's day, to offer unto thee our praises and our prayers, and to hear thy holy word. Thou hast promised to hearken favourably unto all those who call upon thee in the name of thy Son. We therefore beseech thee to look down upon us in mercy, and to purify our thoughts and affections, that we may render unto thee an acceptable service.

Great God! we humble ourselves before thee.

We adore thy majesty; we extol thy wisdom, thy power, and thy goodness, which appear with such brightness in the marvelous works of creation and redemption. We acknowledge thy tender love in the manifold favours, spiritual and temporal, which we continually receive at thy hand; but we praise thee more especially, with all Christians who are assembled this day, that thou didst send thy Son into the world to save us, and that he rose from the dead for our justification. We bless thee that thou hast given us, by his glorious resurrection, so lively a hope of everlasting life.

O God! thy glory is great in all thy churches, and the praise of thy name is heard in all the assemblies of thy saints! May our thanksgivings ascend unto thy throne! Make us worthy to be partakers of the resurrection of the just, and of the glory of the kingdom of heaven, whither Jesus Christ hath entered as our forerunner; where he liveth and reigneth; where he is adored and glorified, with thee and the Holy Ghost, God blessed forever. *Amen.*

O God! who hast given thy Holy Scriptures for our instruction, we beseech thee to enlighten our minds and purify our hearts, that we may worthily read, hear, and meditate upon them, and may understand and receive, as we ought, the things which are therein revealed. Enable thy ministers to declare thy word with purity and clearness, with simplicity and zeal. Render their preaching effectual, through the influence of the Holy Spirit, so that the good seed may be received into our hearts, as into ground well prepared, and bring forth fruit in abundance. Grant that we may be not only hearers, but doers of thy word; and that, living conformably with its divine instructions during the time of our sojourning here, we may attain unto eternal salvation, through Jesus Christ our Lord. *Amen.*

Here may be sung a Psalm or Hymn.

Then the Minister shall say,

HEAR with reverence, the Ten Commandments of the Law of God, as they are written in the 20th chapter of the Book of Exodus.

Here the People rise.

GOD spake all these words, saying, I am the Lord thy God, who brought thee out of the land of Egypt, out of the house of bondage.

I.

Thou shalt have no other gods before me.

II.

Thou shalt not make unto thee any graven image, or any likeness of anything that is in heaven above, or that is in the earth beneath, or that is in the water under the earth. Thou shalt not bow down thyself to them, nor serve them: for I, the Lord thy God, am a jealous God, visiting the iniquity of the fathers upon the children, unto the third and fourth generation of them that hate me; and showing mercy unto thousands of them that love me, and keep my commandments.

III.

Thou shalt not take the name of the Lord thy God in vain: for the Lord will not hold him guiltless that taketh his name in vain.

IV.

Remember the Sabbath day, to keep it holy. Six days shalt thou labour, and do all thy work; but the seventh day is the Sabbath of the Lord thy God: in it thou shalt not do any work; thou, nor thy son, nor thy daughter, thy man-servant, nor thy maid-servant, nor thy cattle, nor the stranger that is within thy gates: for in six days the Lord made heaven and earth, the sea, and all that in them is, and rested the seventh day; wherefore, the Lord blessed the Sabbath day and hallowed it.

V.

Honour thy father and thy mother; that thy days may be long upon the land which the Lord thy God giveth thee.

VI.

Thou shalt not kill.

VII.

Thou shalt not commit adultery.

VIII.

Thou shalt not steal.

IX.

Thou shalt not bear false witness against thy neighbour.

X.

Thou shalt not covet thy neighbour's house; thou shalt not covet thy neighbour's wife; nor his man-servant, nor his maid-servant, nor his ox, nor his ass; nor anything that is thy neighbour's.

HEAR also what our Lord Jesus Christ saith, in the 22d chapter of the Gospel according to St. Matthew.

THOU shalt love the Lord thy God with all thy heart, and with all thy soul, and with all thy mind. This is the first and great commandment.

And the second is like unto it. Thou shalt love thy neighbour as thyself.

On these two commandments hang all the law and the prophets.

DEARLY beloved!

If God enter into judgment with us, in his sight shall no man living be justified. *Psalm cxliii.*, 2.

If we say that we have no sin, we deceive ourselves, and the truth is not in us. *I. John, i.*, 8.

If we confess our sins, he is faithful and just to forgive us our sins, and to cleanse us from all unrighteousness. *I. John, i.*, 9.

The sacrifices of God are a broken spirit; a

broken and a contrite heart he will not despise. *Psalm, li.,* 17.

The wages of sin is death; but the gift of God is eternal life, through Jesus Christ our Lord. *Rom., vi.,* 23.

Him that cometh unto me, saith the Lord, I will in no wise cast out. *St. John, vi.,* 37.

Let us therefore, humbly confess our sins.

O LORD God! Eternal and Almighty Father! we confess before thy Divine Majesty that we are miserable sinners, born in corruption and iniquity, prone to evil, and of ourselves incapable of any good. We acknowledge that we transgress in various ways thy holy commandments, so that we draw down on ourselves, through thy righteous judgment, condemnation and death. We are, O Lord! under heartfelt sorrow for having offended thee; and we implore thy grace to relieve our wretchedness. Vouchsafe, O most gracious God and merciful Father! to have compassion on us, in the name of thy Son Jesus Christ, our Lord. Pardon our sins, give us the graces of the Holy Spirit, and increase them day by day; to the end that, heartily acknowledging our unworthiness, and forsaking our sins, we may be filled with that godly sorrow which worketh repentance unto salvation, and may bring forth fruits of righteousness acceptable to thee; through Jesus Christ, our Lord. *Amen.*

OUR Father, who art in heaven, hallowed be thy name; thy kingdom come; thy will be done on earth, as it is in heaven; give us this day our daily bread; and forgive us our trespasses, as we forgive those who trespass against us; and lead us not into temptation; but deliver us from evil; for thine is the kingdom, and the power, and the glory, for ever and ever. *Amen.*

Then shall be read a Lesson from the Old Testament.

Before reading the Lessons from the Old and New Testaments, the Minister shall announce simply the BOOK *and* CHAPTER; *and after reading them, shall use these words,* HERE ENDETH THE *First, or the Second* LESSON.

After the Lesson from the Old Testament shall be sung the following

DOXOLOGY.

Or a Canticle, Psalm or Hymn, when announced by the Minister.

Here the People rise.

GLORY be to God on high, and on earth peace, good-will towards men. We praise thee, we bless thee, we worship thee, we glorify thee, we give thanks to thee for thy great glory, O Lord God, heavenly King, God the Father Almighty.

O Lord, the only begotten Son, Jesus Christ; O Lord God, Lamb of God, Son of the Father, who takest away the sins of the world, have mercy upon us. Thou, who takest away the sins of the world, have mercy upon us, Thou, who takest away the sins of the world, receive our prayer. Thou, who sittest at the right hand of God the Father, have mercy upon us.

For thou only art holy; thou only art the Lord; thou only, O Christ, with the Holy Ghost, art most high in the glory of God the Father. *Amen.*

Then shall be read a Lesson from the New Testament.

Notice may be given here, if any of the Special or Occasional Prayers, or Thanksgivings, from Part III., are to be used.

After which, the Minister says,

Let us pray.

O LORD! let thy mercy shine upon us; and grant us thy salvation.

O God! make clean our hearts within us; and take not thy Holy Spirit from us.

O LORD God! we render thanks unto thee, that thou hast called us to the knowledge and profession of the Christian faith. We beseech thee to preserve and increase it in us; to the end, that continuing steadfast in the same, we may sincerely unite in the confession of the Church Universal:

I believe in God, the Father Almighty, Creator of heaven and earth.

I believe in Jesus Christ his only Son, our Lord; who was conceived of the Holy Ghost, and born of the Virgin Mary. He suffered under Pontius Pilate; he was crucified; he died; he was buried; [he went into the place of departed spirits;]* the third day he rose from the dead; he ascended into heaven; he sitteth at the right hand of God, the Father Almighty; and thence he will come to judge the living and the dead.

I believe in the Holy Ghost.

I believe in the Holy Church Universal; the communion of saints; the remission of sins; the resurrection of the body; and the life everlasting. *Amen.*

Here introduce such of the Special or Occasional Prayers or Thanksgivings from Part III. as are suitable, may be requested, or the Minister's discretion may suggest.

O LORD, our God! Creator and Father of the human race! who hast commanded that prayer and supplication be made for all mankind, we offer unto thee our intercessions, for the peace of the world, and for the happiness and salvation of all men.

DELIVER, we beseech thee, O Lord! from spiritual blindness, all the nations that still sit in darkness. Thou didst so love the world, that thou gavest thine only Son, to die as a propitiation, not only for our sins, but also for the sins of the whole world. Thou hast taught us that he came to be a light unto the Gentiles, and to bring salvation unto the ends of the

* These words may be omitted.

earth; and that there is none other name under heaven, given among men, whereby we may be saved. Grant, O Almighty God and merciful Father! that all our fellow-men may be gathered unto the name of our Lord; to the end that all nations may know and adore thee, the only true God, and Jesus Christ, whom thou hast sent.

O LORD! who art the source of all lawful power, and the fountain of all true wisdom in the counsels of men, we pray to thee for all who are in authority throughout the world. Thou hast taught us, in thy holy word, that thou dost govern the nations upon earth, and that rulers should serve and obey thee. Vouchsafe, then, O most mighty God! a knowledge of thyself to such as know thee not, and give thy grace unto all, that, ruling in thy fear, they may do justly, love mercy, and walk humbly with thee.

WE beseech thee to behold with thy favour those who, in the order of thy providence, are entrusted with authority throughout our land. Endue them with thy grace, that, in the administration of justice, the preservation of order, the improvement of our laws, and the execution of judgment, their good works may glorify thee.

WE offer unto thee, O Lord! our prayers for the necessities of the Holy Church Universal. Protect, enlarge, and sanctify it more and more. Deliver all churches which suffer persecution. Take away, we beseech thee, the errors and dissensions which disturb thy people, and unite them all in the bonds of truth, of godliness, and of peace. Grant thy blessings to the Churches of these States, and to the families and persons who compose them, that piety, concord, and every Christian virtue may flourish therein.

We pray thee, O Lord! for all the pastors of thy Church. Sanctify them, and increase in them the knowledge and gifts needful for the advancement of thy kingdom, and the salvation of the souls committed to them. Raise up, everywhere, faithful, zealous and humble ministers, lovers of truth and of peace; and, to this end, give thy grace and thy fear to all who are preparing to serve thee in the holy ministry.

O God of mercy! have pity on those who are suffering by war, pestilence, or any other scourge, and on all who are in affliction. We commend to thy care the widow and the orphan, the poor and the stranger, all who are in peril by land or by water, all who endure persecution for the Gospel, all who are distressed in mind, the infirm, the sick and the dying. Comfort and relieve them, according to their several necessities, and give them a happy issue out of all their trials and afflictions.

O Lord! we pray for all thy children. Direct and bless all who seek thee with sincerity of heart, and who labour for the salvation of themselves, or of their fellow-men; all who are engaged in works of love, and in holy designs for the advancement of thy kingdom. Strengthen all who are weak in faith, and in piety, and turn unto thee the hearts of the impenitent and disobedient.

FAVOURABLY regard, O Lord! our country and its inhabitants. Grant, at all times, whatever may be necessary for our subsistence, and give us grace not to abuse thy blessings, but to use them with soberness, charity, and thankfulness.

SAVE us, O merciful God! from all the dangers and calamities to which we may be exposed. Deliver us from our sins; preserve us from every evil thought, from impiety, and hypocrisy, and from all that is contrary to thy holy will. Direct us always by thy grace, and further us continually by thy Spirit. Give unto us, at all times, good and holy thoughts, pure, meek, and peaceable dispositions, entire resignation to thy providence, fervent love to thee, and sincere charity, inclining us to edify and do good to one another. Wean our affections from this world of vanity, and, through thy grace, may our hearts be always lifted up towards heaven. There may our treasure be: to the end that, watching and praying without ceasing, and leading humble, righteous and sober lives, we may pass our days in peace, looking for the glorious advent of our Saviour; at whose coming to judge the world, grant that we, who are here assembled in thy presence, may appear before thee, without confusion and without fear.

FAVOURABLY hear us, O God! Graciously hear all who have at this time offered up their prayers unto thee. Reject not the supplications of thy servants; but grant us the blessings we have asked of thee, and all others which are necessary for us, through Jesus Christ, our Lord, in whose name we offer up our prayers. *Amen.*

Then follow a Psalm or Hymn, the Sermon, a Psalm or Hymn and Doxology, a concluding Prayer, from Part III., and a Benediction.

BENEDICTIONS.

THE Lord bless you and keep you. The Lord make his face shine upon you, and be gracious unto you. The Lord lift up his countenance upon you, and give you peace. *Amen.* *Numb.*, *vi.*, 24, 25, 26.

THE grace of our Lord Jesus Christ, and the love of God, and the communion of the Holy Ghost, be with us all evermore. *Amen.* *II. Cor.*, *xiii.*, 14.

MY brethren! the end of all things is at hand. Be ye therefore sober, and watch unto prayer. *I. Peter*, *iv.*, 7.

The Lord be with you. Almighty God, the Father, the Son, and the Holy Ghost, bless and protect you. *Amen.*

Afternoon Service for the Lord's Day,

AND OTHER OCCASIONS, AT THE DISCRETION OF THE MINISTER.

The Service may commence with one of the following Canticles, unless another Canticle, or a Psalm or Hymn, be specially announced; during which the Minister and People stand.

CANTICLES.

HOW amiable are thy tabernacles, O Lord of Hosts.

My soul desireth, yea, even longeth, to enter into the courts of the Lord. My heart and my flesh rejoice in the living God.

Blessed are they that dwell in thy house: they will be alway praising thee.

One day in thy courts is better than a thousand elsewhere: I would rather be a door-keeper in the house of my God, than to dwell in the tents of ungodliness.

For the Lord God is a sun and a shield: no good thing will he withhold from them that walk uprightly.

O Lord of Hosts! blessed is the man that trusteth in thee.

O God! I will abide in thy tabernacle forever: I will trust in the covert of thy wings.

For thou, O God! hast heard my vows: thou hast given me the heritage of those who fear thy name.

I am ever with thee: thou hast holden me by my right hand.

Thou wilt guide me with thy counsel, and afterward receive me to glory.

Whom have I in heaven but thee? and there is none upon earth that I desire besides thee.

They that forsake thee shall perish: thou wilt destroy all them that corrupt themselves before thee.

But it is good for me to draw near unto God; and to put my trust in the Lord God.

Glory be, etc.

Or this.

O LET us be joyful in the Lord our God. Let us serve the Lord with gladness, and come before his presence with a song.

Know ye that the Lord is God; it is he who hath made us, and not we ourselves; we are his people and the sheep of his pasture.

Enter into his gates with thanksgiving, and into his courts with praise. Be thankful unto him and bless his name.

For the Lord is gracious, his mercy is everlasting, and his truth endureth from generation to generation.

O God! we adore thee as our God, as our Creator, and as the Father of our Lord Jesus Christ.

We humble ourselves in thy presence, and acknowledge thine infinite majesty.

The angels adore thee in heaven, and all the heavenly host bow down before thee.

Receive the homage which we offer to thee upon earth, we who are poor mortals, miserable sinners, thy creatures by nature, and thy children by grace.

Glory be, etc.

Then the Minister shall say,

OUR help is in the name of the Lord, who made heaven and earth.—*Psalm, cxxiv.*, 8.

Here, and at the end of the several Prayers, the People answer

AMEN.

Then the Minister shall say,

DEARLY beloved brethren! we have assembled to worship God, to hear his holy word, and to offer unto him our praises and our prayers. The Father of our Lord Jesus Christ, pardoneth all such as truly repent, and turn unto him.

Let us, therefore, confess our sins, and implore his mercy.

O LORD God! Eternal and Almighty Father! we confess before thy Divine Majesty that we are miserable sinners, born in corruption and iniquity, prone to evil, and of ourselves incapable of any good. We acknowledge that we transgress, in various ways, thy holy commandments, so that we draw down on ourselves, through thy righteous judgment, condemnation and death. We are, O Lord! under heartfelt sorrow for having offended thee; and we implore thy grace to relieve our wretchedness. Vouchsafe, O most gracious God and merciful Father! to have compassion on us, in the name of thy Son Jesus Christ, our Lord. Pardon our sins, give us the graces of the Holy Spirit, and increase them day by day; to the end, that heartily acknowledging our unworthiness, and forsaking our sins, we may be filled with that godly sorrow which worketh repentance unto salvation, and may bring forth fruits of righteousness acceptable to thee; through Jesus Christ, our Lord. *Amen.*

OUR Father, who art in heaven, hallowed be thy name; thy kingdom come; thy will be done on earth, as it is in heaven; give us this day our daily bread; and forgive us our trespasses, as we forgive those who trespass against us; and lead us not into temptation; but deliver us from evil; for thine is the kingdom, and the power, and the glory, for ever and ever. *Amen.*

O MERCIFUL God and heavenly Father! since thou hast given us thy Holy Scriptures as a lamp to our feet, and a light to our paths, we beseech thee, for the love of Jesus Christ, the Light of the world, that thou wouldst illumine our minds, and endue us with the Holy Spirit, to sanctify and lead us into the knowledge of truth. Give us grace to hear attentively thy word, rightly to understand its meaning, and to conform our lives to its precepts; that whatever we shall hear, may tend to the glory of thy name, to our advancement in piety, and to the comfort and salvation of our souls; through Jesus Christ, our Lord. *Amen.*

Then shall be read a Lesson from the Old Testament.

Before reading the Lessons from the Old and New Testaments, the Minister shall announce simply the BOOK *and* CHAPTER; *and after reading them, shall use these words,* HERE ENDETH *the First, or the Second* LESSON.

After the Lesson from the Old Testament, shall be sung the following

DOXOLOGY.

Or a Canticle, Psalm or Hymn, when announced by the Minister.

Here the People rise.

GLORY be to God on high, and on earth peace, good-will towards men. We praise thee, we bless thee, we worship thee, we glorify thee, we give thanks to thee for thy great glory, O Lord God, heavenly King, God the Father Almighty.

O Lord, the only begotten Son, Jesus Christ; O Lord God, Lamb of God, Son of the Father, who takest away the sins of the world, have mercy upon us. Thou, who takest away the sins of the world, have mercy upon us. Thou, who takest away the sins of the world, receive our prayer. Thou, who sittest at the right hand of God the Father, have mercy upon us.

For thou only art holy; thou only art the Lord; thou only, O Christ, with the Holy Ghost, art most high in the glory of God the Father. *Amen.*

Then shall be read a Lesson from the New Testament.

Notice may be given here, if any of the Special or Occasional Prayers, or Thanksgivings, from Part III., are to be used.

After which, the Minister says,

Let us pray.

O LORD! let thy mercy shine upon us; and grant us thy salvation.

O God! make clean our hearts within us; and take not thy Holy Spirit from us.

O LORD God! we render thanks unto thee, that thou hast called us to the knowledge and profession of the Christian faith. We beseech thee to preserve and increase it in us; to the end, that continuing steadfast in the same, we may sincerely unite in the confession of the Church Universal:

I believe in God, the Father Almighty, Creator of heaven and earth.

I believe in Jesus Christ his only Son, our Lord; who was conceived of the Holy Ghost, and born of the Virgin Mary. He suffered under Pontius Pilate;

he was crucified; he died; he was buried; [he went into the place of departed spirits;]* the third day he rose from the dead; he ascended into heaven; he sitteth at the right hand of God, the Father Almighty; and thence he will come to judge the living and the dead.

I believe in the Holy Ghost.

I believe the Holy Church Universal; the communion of saints; the remission of sins; the resurrection of the body; and the life everlasting. *Amen.*

O ALMIGHTY God! Father of mercy! we, thine unworthy servants, do give thee most humble and hearty thanks, for all thy goodness and loving-kindness to us, and to all men. We bless thee for our creation, preservation, and all the blessings of this life; but above all, for thine inestimable love, in the redemption of the world, by our Lord Jesus Christ; for the means of grace, and for the hope of glory. And we beseech thee, give us a due sense of all thy mercies, that we may show forth thy praise, not only with our lips, but in our lives, by giving up ourselves to thy service, and by walking before thee, in holiness and righteousness, all our days; through Jesus Christ our Lord, to whom, with thee, and the Holy Ghost, be all honour and glory, world without end. *Amen.*

Here introduce such of the Special or Occasional Prayers or Thanksgivings from Part III. as are suitable, may be requested, or the Minister's discretion may suggest.

* These words may be omitted.

O ETERNAL and Almighty God! we offer to thy Divine Majesty our prayers for ourselves, and for all mankind.

WE beseech thee to illumine all the people of the earth, by the light of the Gospel, that they may come to the knowledge of the truth, and be saved. We pray thee to provide for all the wants of the Church Universal. Look down with mercy upon all thy people. Preserve them, and cherish in them the light of thy word. Put away from them dissensions and hypocrisy; and grant that piety, charity, and every Christian virtue may reign among them.

BLESS, O God! the ministers of thy church. Enable them at all times, to preach thy word in faithfulness and purity, and to labour with humility and zeal, for the edification of their flocks.

WE pray to thee, King of kings and Lord of lords! for all rulers, and especially for those who are in authority over us. Guide them by thy Spirit, and assist them in the performance of their duties, so that religion, justice and peace may flourish under their government.

O ALMIGHTY and most merciful God! we commend to thy favour all who are in affliction. Grant to the sick the patience, the succour, and the repentance which they need. Convert sinners, and strengthen those who walk in thy ways. O God! bless the just and upright in heart; protect the weak and the innocent; provide for the poor and the stranger; help and comfort all who are in danger, necessity, or tribulation.

BLESS, O God! our country, and all its inhabitants. Turn away from us thy judgments, and be gracious unto us, for the sake of thy Holy name.

VOUCHSAFE, O Lord! to bless us in the duties and business of our several callings. Guide and assist us, that we may always incline to thy will and walk in thy way; that whilst we labour for things temporal, we neglect not things eternal; but that we may first, and chiefly, seek thy kingdom and thy righteousness. Suffer not the temptations and cares of this life to seduce our hearts, and to destroy the seed of thy word, which is sown therein. Teach us, O God! rightly to comprehend that this world passeth away, and all its sinful desires; that our life fleeth as a shadow, and that we bring our years to an end, as it were, a tale that is told. Enable us duly to consider the vanity of this life, so that having lived in thy fear, we may die in thy grace, and be partakers in the resurrection of the just.

O LORD, our gracious God! vouchsafe to us, we beseech thee, all that we need to finish happily the race set before us. Take us under thy protection, provide for all our wants, and guide us, even to our last hour; through Jesus Christ, thy Son. *Amen.*

Then follow a Psalm or Hymn, the Sermon, a Psalm or Hymn and Doxology, a concluding Prayer, from Part III., and a Benediction.

BENEDICTIONS.

THE Lord bless you and keep you. The Lord make his face shine upon you, and be gracious unto you. The Lord lift up his countenance upon you, and give you peace. *Amen.* *Numb.*, *vi.*, 24, 25, 26.

THE grace of our Lord Jesus Christ, and the love of God, and the communion of the Holy Ghost, be with us all evermore. *Amen.* *II. Cor.*, *xiii.*, 14.

MY brethren! the end of all things is at hand. Be ye therefore sober, and watch unto prayer. *I. Peter*, *iv.*, 7.

The Lord be with you. Almighty God, the Father, the Son, and the Holy Ghost, bless and protect you. *Amen.*

PART SECOND.

Morning Service for Week Days, with a Sermon.

The Service may commence with a Canticle, Psalm or Hymn, announced by the Minister.

Then the Minister shall say,

OUR help is in the name of the Lord, who made heaven and earth.—*Psalm*, *cxxiv.*, 8.

Here, and at the end of the several prayers, the People answer

AMEN.

Then the Minister shall say,

DEARLY beloved brethren ! we have assembled to worship God, to hear his holy word, and to offer unto him our praises and our prayers. The Father of our Lord Jesus Christ, pardoneth all such as truly repent, and turn unto him.

Let us, therefore, confess our sins, and implore his mercy.

O LORD, our God and our Father! we are not worthy to appear in thy presence, or to ask of thee any favour. We have not obeyed thy commandments, but have transgressed them in various ways. O Lord! we deplore the magnitude and number of our sins. Pardon us, O most gracious Father! pardon, for the love of Jesus Christ, those who are penitent and ask thy forgiveness. Sanctify us, and make us new creatures; to the end that the glory of thy mercy may be ever manifested in us; through Jesus Christ our Lord. *Amen.*

OUR Father, who art in heaven, hallowed be thy name; thy kingdom come; thy will be done on earth, as it is in heaven; give us this day our daily bread; and forgive us our trespasses, as we forgive those who trespass against us; and lead us not into temptation; but deliver us from evil: for thine is the kingdom, and the power, and the glory, for ever and ever. *Amen.*

IT is meet and proper, that we should adore thee O Lord our God! Creator of heaven and earth, and all things therein, and that we should ever give thanks unto thee for the favours we are continually receiving at thy bountiful hand. We bless thee, that thou hast preserved us to the present time; that, having protected us during the past night, thou hast brought us in safety to the beginning of this day; and that we are enabled to assemble in this holy place, and in thy presence.

O Lord! we praise thee, we desire to serve thee

at this time, and throughout our lives; to dedicate ourselves unto thee, and to submit ourselves entirely to thy holy and gracious will. May it please thee to defend and direct us during this day, that we may pass the same in peace and cheerfulness, in thy fear, and to thy glory.

And, since thou hast given us the Holy Scriptures, as a lamp to our feet and a light to our paths, we beseech thee, O Lord, for the love of Jesus Christ, the Light of the world, that thou wouldst illumine our minds, and endue us with thy Holy Spirit, to sanctify and lead us into the knowledge of truth. Give us grace to hear attentively thy word, rightly to understand its meaning, and to conform our lives to its precepts, so that whatever we shall hear may tend to the glory of thy name, to our advancement in piety, and to the comfort and salvation of our souls; through Jesus Christ our Lord. *Amen.*

Then shall be read a Lesson from the Old Testament.

After which shall be sung the following Doxology; or a Canticle, Psalm or Hymn, when announced by the Minister.

DOXOLOGY.

Here the People rise.

GLORY be to God on high, and on earth peace, good will towards men. We praise thee, we bless thee, we worship thee, we glorify thee, we give thanks to thee for thy great glory, O Lord God, heavenly King, God the Father Almighty.

O Lord, the only begotten Son, Jesus Christ; O Lord God, Lamb of God, Son of the Father, who takest away the sins of the world, have mercy upon us. Thou, who takest away the sins of the world, have mercy upon us. Thou, who takest away the sins of the world, receive our prayer. Thou, who sittest at the right hand of God the Father, have mercy upon us.

For thou only art holy; thou only art the Lord; thou only, O Christ, with the Holy Ghost, art most high in the glory of God the Father. *Amen.*

Then shall be read a Lesson from the New Testament.

Here introduce such of the Special or Occasional Prayers or Thanksgivings, from Part III., as are suitable, may be requested, or the Minister's discretion may suggest.

After which, the Minister says,

Let us pray.

O ETERNAL and Almighty God! we offer to thy Divine Majesty, our prayers for ourselves, and for all mankind.

We beseech thee to illumine all the people of the earth, by the light of the Gospel, that they may come to the knowledge of the truth, and be saved. We pray thee to provide for all the wants of the Church Universal. Look down with mercy upon all thy people. Preserve them, and cherish in them the light of thy word. Put away from them dissensions, and hypocrisy; and grant that piety, charity, and every Christian virtue, may reign among them.

Bless, O God, the ministers of thy church. Enable them, at all times, to preach thy word in faithfulness and purity, and to labour with humility and zeal, for the edification of their flocks.

We pray to thee, King of kings, and Lord of lords! for all rulers, and especially for those who are in authority over us. Guide them by thy Spirit, and assist them in the performance of their duties, so that religion, justice, and peace, may flourish under their government.

O Almighty and most merciful God! we commend to thy favour all who are in affliction. Grant to the sick, the patience, the succour, and the repentance, which they need. Convert sinners, and strengthen those who walk in thy ways. O God! bless the just and upright in heart; protect the weak and the innocent; provide for the poor and the stranger; help and comfort all who are in danger, necessity, or tribulation.

Bless, O God, our country and all its inhabitants. Turn away from us thy judgments, and be gracious unto us, for the sake of thy Holy name.

Vouchsafe, O Lord! to bless us in the duties and business of our several callings. Guide and assist us, that we may always incline to thy will and walk in thy way; that whilst we labour for things temporal, we neglect not things eternal; but that we may first and chiefly seek thy kingdom and thy righteousness. Suffer not the temptations and cares of this life to seduce our hearts, and to destroy the seed of thy word, which is sown therein. Teach us, O God! rightly to comprehend that this world passeth away, and all its sinful desires; that our life fleeth as a shadow, and that we bring our years to an end, as it were a tale that is told. Enable us duly to consider the vanity of this life, so that, having lived in thy fear, we may die in thy grace, and be partakers in the resurrection of the just.

O LORD, our gracious God! vouchsafe to us, we beseech thee, all that we need, to finish happily the race set before us. Take us under thy protection, provide for all our wants, and guide us, even to our last hour; through Jesus Christ thy Son. *Amen.*

Then follow a Psalm or Hymn, the Sermon, a concluding Prayer from Part III., and a Benediction.

BENEDICTIONS.

THE Lord bless you and keep you. The Lord make his face to shine upon you, and be gracious unto you. The Lord lift up his countenance upon you, and give you peace. *Amen.* *Numb., vi.,* 24, 25, 26.

THE grace of our Lord Jesus Christ, the love of God, and the communion of the Holy Ghost, be with us all, evermore. *Amen.* *II. Cor., xiii.,* 14.

MY brethren! the end of all things is at hand. Be ye therefore sober, and watch unto prayer. *I. Peter*, *iv.*, 7.

The Lord be with you. Almighty God, the Father, the Son, and the Holy Ghost, bless and protect you. *Amen.*

Services for Week Days, without a Sermon.

A SERVICE FOR MORNING OR AFTERNOON.

The Service may commence with a Canticle, Psalm or Hymn, announced by the Minister.

Then the Minister shall say,

OUR help is in the name of the Lord, who made heaven and earth. *Psalm, cxxiv.*, 8.

Here, and at the end of the several Prayers, the People answer

AMEN.

Then the Minister shall say,

DEARLY beloved brethren! We have assembled to worship God, to hear his holy word, and to offer unto him our praises and our prayers. The Father of our Lord Jesus Christ pardoneth all such as truly repent, and turn unto him.

Let us, therefore, confess our sins, and implore his mercy.

O ALMIGHTY God! heavenly Father! we have sinned against thee, and are not worthy to be called thy children. We have offended thee in various ways, by thought, word and deed, as thou knowest, O omniscient God! But we pray thee to turn away thine anger from us, forgiving us all our sins, and leading us, by a sincere repentance, to life everlasting, for the love of thy Son, Jesus Christ. *Amen.*

OUR Father, who art in heaven, hallowed be thy name; thy kingdom come; thy will be done on earth, as it is in heaven; give us this day our daily bread; and forgive us our trespasses, as we forgive those who trespass against us; and lead us not into temptation; but deliver us from evil: for thine is the kingdom, and the power, and the glory, for ever and ever. *Amen.*

O MERCIFUL God and heavenly Father! as we are about to hear thy holy word, we pray thee to give us grace rightly to understand its meaning, and to live according to the same, for the love of Jesus Christ, our Saviour. *Amen.*

Then shall be read a Lesson from the Old Testament.

After which shall be sung the following Doxology; or a Canticle, or Psalm or Hymn, when announced by the Minister.

DOXOLOGY.

Here the People rise.

GLORY be to God on high, and on earth peace, good will towards men. We praise thee, we bless thee, we worship thee, we glorify thee, we give thanks to thee for thy great glory, O Lord God, Heavenly King, God the Father Almighty.

O Lord, the only-begotten Son, Jesus Christ; O Lord God, Lamb of God, Son of the Father, who takest away the sins of the world, have mercy upon us. Thou, who takest away the sins of the world, have mercy upon us. Thou, who takest away the sins of the world, receive our prayer. Thou, that sittest at the right hand of God the Father, have mercy upon us.

For thou only art holy; thou only art the Lord; thou only, O Christ, with the Holy Ghost, art most high in the glory of God the Father. *Amen.*

Then shall be read a Lesson from the New Testament.

After which, the Minister says,

Let us pray.

O LORD! have mercy upon us; hear our prayers, and let our supplications come unto thee.

O Lord! let thy mercy shine upon us, and grant us thy salvation.

O Lord, preserve thy Holy Church, and favourably hear, through thy grace, all who call upon thee.

Clothe thy ministers with righteousness, and cause thy chosen people to rejoice.

O Lord! save thy people and bless thine heritage. Grant us peace in our day, for thou only canst defend us.

O God! make clean our hearts within us, and take not thy Holy Spirit from us.

If used in the Morning.

O ETERNAL and Almighty God! we thank thee that thou hast brought us safely to the beginning of this day. Keep us through the same, by thy great power; preserve us from sin, guard us against danger, and so direct us by thy holy guidance, that all our doings may be righteous in thy sight. O Lord! we desire to present ourselves unto thee, a living sacrifice; to consecrate to thee our bodies, our souls, our lives, all that is within us, and all that depends upon us; and to employ them to thy glory. Enable us to resign ourselves unto thy will, O God! to confide in thy providence; and to submit ourselves to all the events which it shall please thee to ordain. Do with us whatsoever shall seem good unto thee; and may thy holy will be done in us and by us; for the love of our Saviour, Jesus Christ. *Amen.*

If used in the Afternoon.

O ETERNAL and Almighty God! we implore thy Divine Majesty to receive the sacrifice of praise which we offer, and to hear the prayers which we address unto thee, at the close of this day. Protect us, we beseech thee, during the night. Preserve us from sin and danger, that we may praise and serve thee at all times. O Lord! we commit our souls to thy care. Guide us whilst awake; guard us whilst we sleep; so that, by day or by night, we may be always with thee; through Jesus Christ, our Lord. *Amen.*

Here introduce such of the Special or Occasional Prayers or Thanksgivings, from Part III., as are suitable, may be requested, or the Minister's discretion may suggest.

O ALMIGHTY God! who hast commanded us to pray for all mankind, and desirest that all may come to a knowledge of the truth, and be saved, favourably hear the supplications which we offer unto thee, for the peace and happiness of all nations, and for the conversion of all who sit in darkness. We implore thy grace for all rulers and magistrates, and especially for the President of the United States, and all others in authority over us. We beseech thee, O God! to preserve and sanctify thy Church, throughout the world, and especially the Church in our own country. Strengthen thou the pastors and ministers of thy word. Have mercy on all nations and persons in affliction. Deliver all who are under persecution, or in captivity, for the sake of the truth. Relieve, comfort and assist the sick and the dying. Vouchsafe unto sinners opportunity and means for repentance and amendment. Strengthen all who are weak in faith and in godliness. Give unto those who love and fear thee, grace to persevere and advance continually in holiness. Bless all who are engaged in works of piety and charity. Grant peace, O Lord! to these

United States. Bless the fruits of the earth. (Bless this city, and all its inhabitants.) Bless all who are here present, and who call upon thee with sincerity of heart. Favourably hear us, O God! Give us grace to pass our days in thy fear, and to end them in thy peace; through Jesus Christ our Lord, who liveth and reigneth with thee and the Holy Spirit, one God, blessed forever. *Amen.*

Or the following Prayer.

ALMIGHTY God! suffer not thy holy name to be reproached on account of our offences. We have sinned against thee in various ways; we have not obeyed thy word as we ought, but have daily provoked thine anger, so that thou mightest justly have punished us. But, O Lord! remember us in mercy, and have compassion on us. Give us grace to be deeply sensible of our sins, to repent of them, and to amend our lives. Bless thy people, O God! Strengthen thy ministers, that they may preach thy word, and exercise their ministry, with faithfulness and zeal. Strengthen, likewise, all rulers and magistrates, that they may use the trust committed to them for thy glory, and the good of thy people. Send down thy blessing on the President of the United States, and on all others in authority over us. O gracious God! turn aside thy judgments from us, and be always our Protector. Confound all designs against thy church, and against thy gospel. O Lord! deprive us not of thy word, and take not thy

Holy Spirit from us; but give us grace to persevere constantly in faith, and in the fear of thy name. Comfort and strengthen all such as are feeble and afflicted, in mind or body. Assist us, O God! in our various necessities, and grant us thy peace; through Jesus Christ our Lord. *Amen.*

ALMIGHTY God! who hast graciously promised to hear the supplications of those who ask in thy Son's name, we beseech thee to accept the service and the prayers, which we have now offered unto thee. May those things which we have faithfully asked, according to thy will, be effectually obtained, for the relief of our necessities, and to the advancement of thy glory; through Jesus Christ our Lord. *Amen.*

Or this.

ALMIGHTY God! who hast given us grace at this time, with one accord, to make our common supplications unto thee; and hast promised that when two or three are gathered together, in thy name, thou wilt grant their requests; fulfil now, O Lord! the desires and petitions of thy servants, as may be most expedient for them, granting us in this world, knowledge of thy truth, and in the world to come, life everlasting. *Amen.*

Here may be sung a Canticle, Psalm or Hymn.

After which shall be said a Benediction.

BENEDICTIONS.

THE Lord bless you and keep you. The Lord make his face to shine upon you, and be gracious unto you. The Lord lift up his countenance upon you, and give you peace. *Amen. Numb., vi.*, 24, 25, 26.

THE grace of our Lord Jesus Christ, the love of God, and the communion of the Holy Ghost, be with us all evermore. *Amen. II. Cor., xiii.*, 14.

MY brethren! the end of all things is at hand. Be ye therefore sober, and watch unto prayer. *I. Peter, iv.*, 7.

The Lord be with you. Almighty God, the Father, the Son, and the Holy Ghost, bless and protect you. *Amen.*

A Service for the Afternoon.

The Service may commence with a Canticle, Psalm or Hymn, announced by the Minister.

Then the Minister shall say,

OUR help is in the name of the Lord, who made heaven and earth. *Psalm, cxxiv.*, 8.

Here, and at the end of the several Prayers, the People answer

AMEN.

Then the Minister shall say,

DEARLY beloved brethren! we have assembled to worship God, to hear his holy word, and to offer unto him our praises and our prayers. The Father of our Lord Jesus Christ pardoneth all such as truly repent, and turn unto him.

Let us, therefore, confess our sins, and implore his mercy.

O ALMIGHTY God! Heavenly Father! we have sinned against thee, and are nôt worthy to be called thy children. We have offended thee in various ways, by thought, word and deed, as thou knowest, O omniscient God! But we pray thee to turn away thine anger from us; forgiving us all our sins, and leading us, by a sincere repentance, to life everlasting, for the love of thy Son, Jesus Christ. *Amen.*

OUR Father, who art in heaven, hallowed be thy name; thy kingdom come; thy will be done on earth, as it is in heaven; give us this day our daily bread; and forgive us our trespasses, as we forgive those who trespass against us; and lead us not into temptation; but deliver us from evil; for thine is the kingdom, and the power, and the glory, for ever and ever. *Amen.*

O MERCIFUL God and Heavenly Father! as we are about to hear thy holy word, we pray thee to give us grace rightly to understand its meaning, and to live according to the same, for the love of Jesus Christ our Saviour. *Amen.*

Then shall be read a Lesson from the Old Testament.

After which shall be sung the following Doxology; or a Canticle, Psalm or Hymn, when announced by the Minister.

DOXOLOGY.

Here the People rise.

GLORY be to God on high, and on earth peace, good will towards men. We praise thee, we bless thee, we worship thee, we glorify thee, we give thanks to thee for thy great glory, O Lord God, heavenly King, God the Father Almighty.

O Lord, the only begotten Son, Jesus Christ; O Lord God, Lamb of God, Son of the Father, who takest away the sins of the world, have mercy upon us. Thou, who takest away the sins of the world, have mercy upon us. Thou, who takest away the sins of the world, receive our prayer. Thou, who sittest at the right hand of God the Father, have mercy upon us.

For thou only art holy; thou only art the Lord; thou only, O Christ, with the Holy Ghost, art most high in the glory of God the Father. *Amen.*

Then shall be read a Lesson from the New Testament.

After which, the Minister says,

Let us pray.

O LORD! have mercy upon us; hear our prayers, and let our supplications come unto thee.

O Lord! let thy mercy shine upon us; and grant us thy salvation.

O Lord! preserve thy Holy Church, and favourably hear, through thy grace, all who call upon thee.

Clothe thy ministers with righteousness, and cause thy chosen people to rejoice.

O Lord! save thy people and bless thine heritage. Grant us peace in our day, for thou only canst defend us.

O God! make clean our hearts within us, and take not thy Holy Spirit from us.

O LORD God! we render thanks unto thee, that thou hast called us to the knowledge and profession of the Christian faith. We beseech thee to preserve and increase it in us; to the end, that continuing steadfast in the same, we may sincerely unite in the confession of the Church Universal:

I believe in God, the Father Almighty, Creator of heaven and earth.

I believe in Jesus Christ, his only Son, our Lord; who was conceived of the Holy Ghost, and born of the Virgin Mary. He suffered under Pontius Pilate; he was crucified; he died; he was buried; [he went into the place of departed spirits;]* the third day he rose from the dead; he ascended into heaven; he sitteth at the right hand of God, the Father Almighty; and thence he will come to judge the living and the dead.

I believe in the Holy Ghost.

I believe the Holy Church Universal; the communion of saints; the remission of sins; the resurrection of the body; and the life everlasting. *Amen.*

O ALMIGHTY God! Father of mercy! we, thine unworthy servants, do give thee most humble and hearty thanks, for all thy goodness and loving-kindness to us, and to all men. We bless thee for our creation, preservation, and all the blessings of this life; but above all, for thine inestimable love, in the redemption of the world, by our Lord Jesus Christ; for the means of grace, and for the hope of

* These words may be omitted.

glory. And we beseech thee, give us a due sense of all thy mercies, that we may show forth thy praise, not only with our lips, but in our lives, by giving up ourselves to thy service, and by walking before thee, in holiness and righteousness, all our days; through Jesus Christ our Lord, to whom, with thee, and the Holy Spirit, be all honour and glory, world without end. *Amen.*

O LORD! who art the God of peace, and the author of all good, grant unto thy servants that peace which the world cannot give, that our hearts may be inclined to obey thy commandments, and that, being delivered from the fear of our enemies, we may pass our lives in rest and quietness, through the merits of Jesus Christ, our Saviour. *Amen.*

O LORD! watch over us, and, through thy great mercy, defend our souls and bodies from all danger during the coming night; for the love of thine only Son our Saviour, Jesus Christ.

Here introduce such of the Special or Occasional Prayers or Thanksgivings from Part III. as are suitable, may be requested, or the Minister's discretion may suggest.

O GOD! who art King of kings, and Lord of lords, we beseech thee favourably to look upon all rulers and magistrates, and to send down thy blessings upon the President of these United States, and on all others in authority over us. Give them grace to live to the advancement of thy glory, the good of thy church, and the welfare of our country; through Jesus Christ, our Redeemer. *Amen.*

ALMIGHTY and Everlasting God! send down upon our pastors, upon all thy ministers, and upon the congregations committed to their charge, the healthful spirit of thy grace. Fill thy servants so abundantly with the knowledge of thy truth, and so clothe them with innocence of life, that they may exercise their ministry to the glory of thy name, and to the edification of thy holy Church, through Jesus Christ, our Lord. *Amen.*

O GOD! the Creator and Preserver of all mankind, we humbly beseech thee for all sorts and conditions of men, that thou wouldst be pleased to make thy ways known unto them, thy saving health unto all nations. We pray to thee especially for the prosperity of the Church Universal, that it may be so governed by thy Spirit, that all who profess and call themselves Christians may be led into the way of truth, and hold the faith in unity of spirit, in the bond of peace, and in righteousness of life. Finally, we commend to thy fatherly goodness all who are distressed in mind, body or estate; that it may please thee to comfort and relieve them, according to their several necessities, giving them repentance and patience under their sufferings, and a happy issue out of all their afflictions. All these things we ask of thee for the love of Jesus Christ. *Amen.*

ALMIGHTY God! who hast given us grace at this time, with one accord, to make our common supplications unto thee; and hast promised that when two or three are gathered together in thy name, thou wilt grant their requests; fulfil now, O Lord! the desires and petitions of thy servants, as may be most expedient for them, granting us, in this world, knowledge of thy truth, and in the world to come, life everlasting. *Amen.*

Here may be sung a Canticle, Psalm or Hymn.

After which shall be said a Benediction.

BENEDICTIONS.

THE Lord bless you and keep you. The Lord make his face shine upon you, and be gracious unto you. The Lord lift up his countenance upon you, and give you peace. *Amen. Numb. vi.*, 24, 25, 26.

THE grace of our Lord Jesus Christ, and the love of God, and the communion of the Holy Ghost, be with us all evermore. *Amen. II. Cor.*, *xiii.*, 14.

MY brethren! the end of all things is at hand. Be ye therefore sober, and watch unto prayer. *I. Peter, iv.*, 7.

The Lord be with you. Almighty God, the Father, the Son, and the Holy Ghost, bless and protect you. *Amen.*

Service for Days of Public Humiliation.

The Service may commence with a Canticle, Psalm or Hymn, announced by the Minister, during which Minister and People stand.

Then the Minister shall say,

OUR help is in the name of the Lord, who made heaven and earth. *Psalm cxxiv.*, 8.

Here, and at the end of the several Prayers, the People answer

AMEN.

Then the Minister shall say,

Let us pray.

O ALMIGHTY God and Merciful Father! into whose presence we have come to offer the sacrifice of repentance and prayer, in the observance of this day of public humiliation, dispose our hearts to sincere and deep self-abasement. Thou art full of compassion, slow to anger, and of great kindness: favourably hear our prayers, and those of our brethren, who now call upon thee; through Jesus Christ, thy Son. *Amen.*

WE beseech thee, O Lord! to give us grace, now and at all times, to hear thy holy word with attention, with reverence, and with fear; and to receive willingly the instructions and admonitions which may be addressed to us by the ministry of thy servants. Vouchsafe to them thine especial help; and grant that they labour not in vain. Let not thy word return to thee unfruitful. May it please thee to accompany it with the power and efficacy of thy Holy Spirit; through Jesus Christ, our Lord. *Amen.*

Then the Minister shall say,

HEAR with reverence, the Ten Commandments of the Law of God, as they are written in the 20th chapter of the Book of Exodus.

Here the People rise.

GOD spake these words, saying, I am the Lord thy God, who brought thee out of the land of Egypt, out of the house of bondage.

I.

Thou shalt have no other gods before me.

II.

Thou shalt not make unto thee any graven image, or any likeness of any thing that is in heaven above, or that is in the earth beneath, or that is in the water under the earth. Thou shalt not bow down thyself to them, nor serve them: for I, the Lord thy God, am a jealous God, visiting the iniquity of the fathers upon the children, unto the third and fourth generation of them that hate me; and showing mercy unto thousands of them that love me, and keep my commandments.

III.

Thou shalt not take the name of the Lord thy God in vain: for the Lord will not hold him guiltless that taketh his name in vain.

IV.

Remember the Sabbath day, to keep it holy. Six days shalt thou labour, and do all thy work; but the seventh day is the Sabbath of the Lord thy God: in it thou shalt not do any work; thou, nor thy son, nor thy daughter, thy man-servant, nor thy maid-servant, nor thy cattle, nor the stranger that is within thy gates: for in six days the Lord made heaven and earth, the sea, and all that in them is, and rested the seventh day; wherefore, the Lord blessed the Sabbath day and hallowed it.

V.

Honour thy father and thy mother; that thy days may be long upon the land which the Lord thy God giveth thee.

VI.

Thou shalt not kill.

VII.

Thou shalt not commit adultery.

VIII.

Thou shalt not steal.

IX.

Thou shalt not bear false witness against thy neighbour.

X.

Thou shalt not covet thy neighbour's house; thou shalt not covet thy neighbour's wife; nor his man-servant, nor his maid-servant, nor his ox, nor his ass; nor anything that is thy neighbour's.

HEAR also what our Lord Jesus Christ saith, in the 22d chapter of the Gospel according to St. Matthew.

THOU shalt love the Lord thy God with all thy heart, and with all thy soul, and with all thy mind. This is the first and great commandment.

And the second is like unto it. Thou shalt love thy neighbour as thyself.

On these two commandments hang all the law and the prophets.

DEARLY beloved!

There is not a just man upon earth, that doeth good and sinneth not. *Ecc. vii.* 20.

If we say we are perfect, it shall also prove us perverse. *Job ix.*, 20.

But there is forgiveness with God. *Psalm cxxx.*, 4.

He hath raised up his Son Jesus, and sent him to bless us, in turning away every one of us from his iniquities. *Acts*, *iii.*, 26.

By prayer and supplication, with thanksgiving,

let our requests be made known unto God. *Philip. iv.*, 6.

Let us pray.

O ALMIGHTY God! Lord of heaven and earth, we humble ourselves before thy Divine Majesty. Thou art God over all, the Supreme, the Eternal. Thou didst make the heavens, and all the hosts thereof; the earth, and all that therein is. Thou givest life to all things; and the army of heaven boweth down before thee. Thy majesty is incomprehensible; thy greatness infinitely above our thoughts and our praises. But thy goodness is over all thy works, and we offer unto thee our thanks for the manifold blessings thou hast vouchsafed to us, even unto this day.

O LORD! we are crowned with thy favours; and the testimonies of thy loving-kindness are ever around us. Thou hast given us life; and thy bountiful hand hath not ceased to provide all that is necessary, to enable us to pass our days in peace. But we praise thee, especially, that thou hast blessed us with all spiritual blessings in Jesus Christ, and art willing to number us with those who have been ransomed by the blood of thy Son, and are called to inherit the glory of thy kingdom. Through thy great mercy, thou hast offered to all of us the means of salvation, furthering us by thy word, by the influence of thy Spirit, by the voice of thy servants, by thy bounties, thy chastisements, and thy continued help. Thou hast not rejected us in the midst of our iniquities; we are this day engaged in thy worship; and thou art still disposed to bless us.

BUT we have abused thy mercies, O our God! and have made them the occasions of transgressing. We have not served thee, even whilst receiving thy benefits. We have not walked in the light of thy Gospel, nor have we lived in a manner worthy of our vocation.

O LORD! we confess the multitude and greatness of our iniquities. Neither we, nor our rulers, nor our pastors, nor the people, have been mindful of thy commandments, nor of the warnings vouchsafed unto us during the years of thy forbearance. O Lord! the sins committed among us provoke thine anger. Impiety and indevotion, hypocrisy, blasphemy, and the profanation of thy holy name, of thy worship, and of thy laws; injustice, violence and fraud; hatred, dissensions, envy and evil speaking; sensuality and intemperance; pride, luxury, avarice, and the love of the world; open transgressions, and secret sins; the trespasses of the high, and the trespasses of the low; all these sins, O God! most righteous judge, all these sins pollute our country and its inhabitants, and justly kindle thine indignation and thy wrath.

O LORD! thou art just, and we are wicked. To thee belongeth righteousness; to us confusion of face. Thou mayest justly condemn us, and cast us away from thy presence; but we confess our guilt, and humbly trust to the greatness of thy mercy.

O God! who desirest not the death of a sinner, but rather that he may turn from his wickedness and live; who despisest not the prayers and sighs of such as call upon thee, hearken unto us, and to all who confess their faults. Give thy grace unto those who are penitent. Turn us unto thee, that, forsaking our sins and living in newness of life, we may be acceptable in thy sight.

O Lord our God! we ask these blessings through thine infinite goodness, in the name of thy Son, our Redeemer, who hath taught us to pray unto thee, saying:—

OUR Father, who art in heaven, hallowed be thy name; thy kingdom come; thy will be done on earth, as it is in heaven; give us this day our daily bread; and forgive us our trespasses, as we forgive those who trespass against us; and lead us not into temptation; but deliver us from evil: for thine is the kingdom, and the power, and the glory, for ever and ever. *Amen.*

Then shall be read a Lesson from the Old Testament.

Before reading the Lessons from the Old and New Testaments, the Minister shall announce the BOOK *and* CHAPTER; *and after reading them, shall use these words,* HERE ENDETH *the First, or the Second* LESSON.

After the Lesson from the Old Testament, shall be sung the following

DOXOLOGY.

Or a Canticle, Psalm or Hymn, announced by the Minister.

Here the People rise.

GLORY be to God on high, and on earth peace, good will towards men. We praise thee, we bless thee, we worship thee, we glorify thee, we give thanks to thee for thy great glory, O Lord God, heavenly King, God the Father Almighty.

O Lord, the only begotten Son, Jesus Christ; O Lord God, Lamb of God, Son of the Father, who takest away the sins of the world, have mercy upon us. Thou, who takest away the sins of the world, have mercy upon us. Thou, who takest away the sins of the world, receive our prayer. Thou, who sittest at the right hand of God the Father, have mercy upon us.

For thou only art holy; thou only art the Lord; thou only, O Christ, with the Holy Ghost, art most high in the glory of God the Father. *Amen.*

Then shall be read a Lesson from the New Testament.

After which, may be sung a Psalm or Hymn.

Then the Sermon, a Psalm or Hymn, and a Doxology.

If any of the Prayers or Thanksgivings from Part III. are to be used, notice may be given here.

Then the Minister shall say,

Let us pray.

Here introduce the Prayers or Thanksgivings from Part III., appropriate to the notice given.

After which, the prayer following, and a Benediction.

O LORD, our God! Creator and Father of the human race! who hast commanded that prayer and supplication be made for all mankind, we beseech thee that the light of thy holy Gospel may shine upon all nations and upon all men, who still sit in darkness, to the end that thy name, which is great and holy, may be known and glorified in all places; through Jesus Christ our Lord.

WE pray to thee, O God! for the prosperity of the Church Universal. Guide it always by thy word and Spirit; and suffer not the gates of hell to prevail against it. Deliver all Churches which suffer persecution. Take away, we beseech thee, the errors and dissensions which disturb thy people; and unite them all in the bonds of truth, of godliness, and of peace. Vouchsafe thy blessing to the Churches of these States; preserve them from error and from vice; remove from them ignorance and scandal; and grant that peace, order and piety may prevail among them. O Lord! be gracious unto this Church, and increase in us the knowledge and the fear of thy name.

WE commend to thy favour, O God! all pastors and ministers, who have been ordained to lead thy flocks. Sanctify and endue plenteously with thy gifts, those who exercise the holy ministry, and those who are preparing for it; and send forth always faithful labourers into thy harvest. Grant success to the pious designs and holy efforts of all thy servants, who seek thy glory and the edification of thy church. Purify thy sanctuary, and rekindle the zeal of pastors and people; that thy holy name may be more and more glorified among us.

WE offer also unto thee our prayers for all rulers and magistrates. Give them a knowledge of thyself, and inspire them with true zeal for thy glory and the good of thy church. We pray for thy blessing on the President of these United States, and on all in authority over us. Guide them in the discharge of their respective duties, and grant that they may have constantly in view the advancement of the public good.

O GOD! continue to watch over our country, and to bless us. Withdraw not thy grace from the people of these States. Turn away from us thy judgments, and be favorable unto us, for the sake of thy holy name.

WE implore thy grace for all who are in tribulation. We commend, especially, to thy mercy all those who are under the cross, and who suffer persecution for righteousness' sake. Comfort and deliver them; raise up those who are fallen; and strengthen all, that they may glorify thee in life and in death. Pity and relieve all who are troubled in mind, body, or estate. Grant them repentance and resignation, and grace to make a right use of their afflictions.

FINALLY, we beseech thee, O Lord! to hear the

prayers, and accept the praises, which have this day been offered up unto thee; and give us, we pray thee, a due sense of all thy mercies, that we may show forth thy praise, not only with our lips, but in our lives; by giving up ourselves to thy service, and by walking before thee, in holiness and righteousness, all our days; through Jesus Christ our Lord, to whom, with thee and the Holy Ghost, be all honour and glory, world without end. *Amen.*

BENEDICTIONS.

THE Lord bless you and keep you. The Lord make his face shine upon you, and be gracious unto you. The Lord lift up his countenance upon you, and give you peace. *Amen. Numb. vi.*, 24, 25, 26.

THE grace of our Lord Jesus Christ, and the love of God, and the communion of the Holy Ghost, be with us all evermore. *Amen. II. Cor.*, *xiii.*, 14.

MY brethren! the end of all things is at hand. Be ye therefore sober, and watch unto prayer. *I. Peter*, *iv.*, 7.

The Lord be with you. Almighty God, the Father, the Son, and the Holy Ghost, bless and protect you. *Amen.*

Service for Days of Public Thanksgiving.

The Service may commence with a Canticle, Psalm or Hymn, announced by the Minister, during which Minister and People stand.

Then the Minister shall say,

OUR help is in the name of the Lord, who made heaven and earth. *Psalm cxxiv.*, 8.

Here, and at the end of the several Prayers, the People answer

AMEN.

Then the Minister shall say,

Let us pray.

O ALMIGHTY God and heavenly Father! we have come together on this day of public thanksgiving, to offer unto thee our praises and our prayers, and to hear thy holy word. Thou hast promised to hearken favourably unto all those who call upon thee in the name of thy Son. We, therefore, beseech thee to look down upon us in mercy, and to purify our thoughts and affections, that we may render unto thee an acceptable service; through Jesus Christ, our Lord. *Amen.*

O GOD! who hast given thy Holy Scriptures for our instruction, we beseech thee to enlighten our minds and purify our hearts, that we may worthily read, hear, and meditate upon them, and may understand and receive, as we ought, the things which are therein revealed. Enable thy ministers to declare thy word with purity and clearness, with simplicity and zeal. Render their preaching effectual, through the influence of the Holy Spirit, so that the good seed may be received into our hearts as into ground well prepared, and bring forth fruit in abundance. Grant that we may be not only hearers, but doers of thy word, and that, living conformably with its divine instructions, during the time of our sojourning here, we may attain unto eternal salvation; through Jesus Christ our Lord. *Amen.*

Here may be sung a Psalm or Hymn.

Then the Minister shall say,

HEAR, with reverence, the Ten Commandments of the Law of God, as they are written in the 20th chapter of the Book of Exodus.

Here the People rise.

GOD spake these words, saying, I am the Lord thy God, who brought thee out of the land of Egypt, out of the house of bondage.

I.

Thou shalt have no other gods before me.

II.

Thou shalt not make unto thee any graven image, or any likeness of any thing that is in heaven above, or that is in the earth beneath, or that is in the water under the earth. Thou shalt not bow down thyself to them, nor serve them: for I, the Lord thy God, am a jealous God, visiting the iniquity of the fathers upon the children, unto the third and fourth generation of them that hate me; and showing mercy unto thousands of them that love me, and keep my commandments.

III.

Thou shalt not take the name of the Lord thy God in vain: for the Lord will not hold him guiltless that taketh his name in vain.

IV.

Remember the Sabbath day, to keep it holy. Six days shalt thou labour, and do all thy work; but the seventh day is the Sabbath of the Lord thy God: in it thou shalt not do any work; thou, nor thy son, nor thy daughter, thy man-servant, nor thy maid-servant, nor thy cattle, nor the stranger that is within thy gates: for in six days the Lord made heaven and earth, the sea, and all that in them is, and rested the seventh day; wherefore, the Lord blessed the Sabbath day and hallowed it.

V.

Honour thy father and thy mother; that thy days

may be long upon the land which the Lord thy God giveth thee.

VI.

Thou shalt not kill.

VII.

Thou shalt not commit adultery.

VIII.

Thou shalt not steal.

IX.

Thou shalt not bear false witness against thy neighbour.

X.

Thou shalt not covet thy neighbour's house; thou shalt not covet thy neighbour's wife; nor his man-servant, nor his maid-servant, nor his ox, nor his ass; nor anything that is thy neighbour's.

HEAR also what our Lord Jesus Christ saith, in the 22d chapter of the Gospel according to St. Matthew.

THOU shalt love the Lord thy God with all thy heart, and with all thy soul, and with all thy mind. This is the first and great commandment.

And the second is like unto it. Thou shalt love thy neighbour as thyself.

On these two commandments hang all the law and the prophets.

DEARLY beloved!

If we say that we have no sin, we deceive ourselves, and the truth is not in us. *I. John, i.*, 8.

If God enter into judgment with us, in his sight shall no man living be justified. *Psalm cxliii.*, 2.

But there is forgiveness with him. *Psalm cxxx*, 4.

If we confess our sins, he is faithful and just to forgive us our sins, and to cleanse us from all unrighteousness. *I. John, i.*, 9.

The sacrifices of God are a broken spirit; a broken and a contrite heart he will not despise. *Psalm li.*, 17.

Him that cometh unto me, saith the Lord, I will in no wise cast out. *St. John vi.*, 37.

Let us, therefore, humbly confess our sins.

O LORD God! Eternal and Almighty Father! we confess before thy Divine Majesty that we are miserable sinners, born in corruption and iniquity, prone to evil, and of ourselves incapable of any good. We acknowledge that we transgress, in various ways, thy holy commandments, so that we draw down on ourselves, through thy righteous judgment, condemnation and death. We are, O Lord! under heartfelt sorrow for having offended thee; and we implore thy grace to relieve our wretchedness. Vouchsafe, O most gracious God and merciful Father! to have compassion on us, in the name of thy Son Jesus Christ our Lord. Pardon our sins, give us the graces of the Holy Spirit, and increase them day by day; to the end, that heartily acknowledging our unworthiness, and forsaking our sins, we may be filled with that godly sorrow which worketh repentance unto salvation, and may bring forth fruits of righteousness acceptable to thee; through Jesus Christ our Lord. *Amen.*

OUR Father, who art in heaven, hallowed be thy name; thy kingdom come; thy will be done on earth, as it is in heaven; give us this day our daily bread; and forgive us our trespasses, as we forgive those who trespass against us; and lead us not into temptation; but deliver us from evil: for thine is the kingdom, and the power, and the glory, for ever and ever. *Amen.*

Then shall be read a Lesson from the Old Testament.

After which shall be sung the following

DOXOLOGY.

Or a Canticle, Psalm, or Hymn, announced by the Minister.

Here the People rise.

GLORY be to God on high, and on earth peace, good will towards men. We praise thee, we bless thee, we worship thee, we glorify thee, we give thanks to thee for thy great glory, O Lord God, heavenly King, God the Father Almighty.

O Lord, the only begotten Son, Jesus Christ; O Lord God, Lamb of God, Son of the Father, that takest away the sins of the world, have mercy upon us. Thou, that takest away the sins of the world, have mercy upon us. Thou, that takest away the sins of the world, receive our prayer. Thou that sittest at the right hand of God the Father, have mercy upon us.

For thou only art holy; thou only art the Lord; thou only, O Christ, with the Holy Ghost, art most high in the glory of God the Father. *Amen.*

Then shall be read a Lesson from the New Testament.

If any of the Prayers or Thanksgivings from Part III. are to be used, notice may be given here.

Then the Minister shall say,

Let us pray.

Here introduce the Prayers or Thanksgivings from Part III., appropriate to the notice given.

After which, as follows.

O GOD! of infinite wisdom, power and goodness, we acknowledge thee as the Creator of all things in the heavens above, in the earth beneath, and in the paths of the sea. We adore thee for the grandeur and beauty of all thy works. We adore thy loving-kindness, in having made them subservient to the wants and happiness of thy children. What is man, that thou art mindful of him, and the son of man, that thou visitest him! Thou hast given him dominion over the fish of the sea, and over the fowls of the air, and over every living thing that moveth upon the earth. Thou hast given to him for meat every moving thing that liveth, and every herb yielding seed, and every fruit tree yielding fruit, after its kind. Thou hast crowned us with mercy and loving-kindness.

We adore thee for thy gracious promise of old, that while the earth remaineth, seed time and harvest, and cold and heat, and summer and winter, and day and night, shall not cease. Thou visitest the earth and blessest it. Thou sendest the springs into the valleys which run among the hills. Thou causest the grass to grow for all cattle, and herb for the service of man, that he may bring forth food out of the earth. Thou makest the furrows of the field soft with showers; thou blessest the springing thereof. The pastures are clothed with flocks; the valleys also are covered over with corn; they shout for joy. Thou crownest the year with thy goodness; thy clouds drop fatness; they drop upon the pastures of the wilderness, and the little hills rejoice on every side. O Lord! how manifold are thy works! in wisdom hast thou made them all.

We would adore thee, O God! not only in the riches of thy bounty and compassion, but in thy righteous judgments. Thou openest thine hand, and we are filled with good; thou hidest thy face, and we are troubled. But we know, O God! that in thy wrath thou rememberest mercy; and we acknowledge thy long-suffering and thy loving-kindness. Give us grace to believe and feel, that whom the Lord loveth he chasteneth; and make us ever ready to offer unto thee, in spirit and in truth, the prayer of the holy prophet: Although the fig tree shall not blossom, neither shall fruit be in the vines, the labour of the olive shall fail, and the fields shall yield no meat; the flock shall be cut off from the fold, and there shall be no herd in the stalls; yet we will rejoice in the Lord, we will joy in the God of our salvation.

For ourselves and our country, O gracious God! we thank thee, that notwithstanding our manifold transgressions of thy holy laws, thou hast so constantly done good to us; that thou hast given us rain from heaven, and fruitful seasons, filling our hearts with food and gladness. These have been among the witnesses of thy great goodness, for they certify of thee that thou art the living God. Teach us to believe with a strong faith, that thou art Lord of the seasons; that thou biddest the earth to bring forth, and it obeyeth thee. Accept our thanksgivings for all the blessings of the year now drawing to a close; fill our hearts with humility and love, with gratitude and trust; continue thy loving-kindness to us, and assist us to show forth the fruits of grace, in a sincere obedience to his will, through whom all blessings are vouchsafed, thy Son our Saviour, Jesus Christ. *Amen.*

Here may be sung a Psalm or Hymn.

Then the Sermon, a Psalm or Hymn, and a Doxology.

After which the following Prayer and a Benediction.

Let us pray.

O LORD our God! Creator and Father of the human race, who hast commanded that prayer and supplication be made for all mankind, we beseech thee that the light of the holy Gospel may shine upon all nations and upon all men, who still sit in darkness, to the end that thy name, which is great and holy, may be known and glorified in all places, through Jesus Christ our Lord.

WE pray to thee, O Lord! for the prosperity of the Church Universal. Guide it always by thy word and Spirit, and suffer not the gates of hell to prevail against it. Deliver all Churches which suffer persecution. Take away, we beseech thee, the errors and dissensions which disturb thy people; and unite them all in the bonds of truth, of godliness, and of peace. Vouchsafe thy blessing to the Churches of these States; preserve them from error and from vice; remove from them ignorance and scandal; and grant that peace, order and piety may prevail among them. O Lord! be gracious unto this Church, and increase in us the knowledge and the fear of thy name.

WE commend to thy favour, O God! all pastors and ministers, who have been ordained to lead thy flocks. Sanctify and endue plenteously with thy gifts, those who exercise the holy ministry, and those who are preparing for it; and send forth always faithful labourers into thy harvest. Grant success to the pious designs and holy efforts of all thy servants, who seek thy glory and the edification of thy church. Purify thy sanctuary, and rekindle the zeal of pastors and people; that thy holy name may be more and more glorified among us.

WE offer also unto thee our prayers for all rulers and magistrates. Give them a knowledge of thyself, and inspire them with true zeal for thy glory and the good of thy church. We pray for thy blessing on the President of these United States, and on all in authority over us. Guide them in the discharge of their respective duties, and grant that they may have constantly in view the advancement of the public good.

O GOD! continue to watch over our country, and to bless us. Withdraw not thy grace from the people of these States. Turn away from us thy judgments, and be favourable unto us, for the sake of thy holy name.

WE implore thy grace for all who are in tribulation. We commend, especially, to thy mercy all those who are under the cross, and who suffer persecution for righteousness' sake. Comfort and deliver them; raise up those who are fallen; and strengthen all, that they may glorify thee in life and in death. Pity and relieve all who are troubled in mind, body, or estate. Grant them repentance and resignation, and grace to make a right use of their afflictions.

FINALLY, we beseech thee, O Lord! to hear the prayers, and accept the praises, which have this day been offered up unto thee; and give us, we pray thee, a due sense of all thy mercies, that we may show forth thy praise, not only with our lips, but in our lives; by giving up ourselves to thy service, and by walking before thee in holiness and righteousness all our days; through Jesus Christ our Lord, to whom, with thee and the Holy Ghost, be all honour and glory, world without end. *Amen.*

BENEDICTIONS.

THE Lord bless you and keep you. The Lord make his face to shine upon you, and be gracious unto you. The Lord lift up his countenance upon you, and give you peace. *Amen. Numbers, vi.*, 24, 25, 26.

THE grace of our Lord Jesus Christ, the love of God, and the communion of the Holy Ghost, be with us all evermore. *Amen. II. Cor., xiii.*, 14.

MY brethren! the end of all things is at hand. Be ye therefore sober, and watch unto prayer. *I. Peter, iv.*, 7.

The Lord be with you. Almighty God, the Father, the Son, and the Holy Ghost, bless and protect you. *Amen.*

PART THIRD.

SECTION FIRST.

Prayers for Stated Occasions.

TO BE USED AS PART OF THE MORNING SERVICE.

For the Day of the Nativity.

O ALMIGHTY God! merciful Father! it is our duty to bless thee, and to give thee thanks at all times, but more especially on this day, when we commemorate the blessed nativity of Jesus Christ, our Redeemer.

Thou hadst promised to our first parents in Paradise, to send thy Son into the world. Thou hadst ordained his coming to be announced by the prophets; and thou didst cause him to be born in the fulness of time. Thine eternal Son, who, from the beginning, was with thee, vouchsafed to take upon him our nature, and to become man; so that he is very God and very man, our Immanuel, God with us. He who was in the form of God, took upon him the form of a servant. He partook, as children do, of our nature, even of our flesh and blood. He was made like unto his brethren in all things, yet without sin, to the end that he might be a merciful high priest, to make reconciliation for our sins.

How great is this mystery of godliness! God manifest in the flesh, justified in the spirit, seen of angels, preached unto the Gentiles, believed on in the world, and received up into glory!

O God! we believe and confess, to the praise of thy mercy, that it is through the coming of thy Son into the world that we do not perish eternally. May our prayers and thanksgivings, on this solemn occasion, be acceptable unto thee! Favourably look upon thy people, who offer unto thee their supplications. Preserve thy church, which this day commemorates the Advent of the Redeemer, and celebrates thy praises.

O God! heavenly Father! who didst send the angel Gabriel to announce the birth of thy Son, Jesus Christ, and didst cause him to be born of the holy Virgin, through the power of the Holy Spirit; sanctify us by the same Spirit, that Christ may be formed in us, that he may live in us and dwell in us by faith, that we may live only in him, and for him.

O LORD! who didst cause a miraculous splendour to shine around the shepherds, on the night in which thy Son came into the world, illumine our minds, we beseech thee, with thy celestial light. So assist us by thy grace, O heavenly Father! that we may live henceforth, even unto the end, as becometh those who believe that thy Son came to save them; and may await with joy and in peace, the glorious appearing of Jesus Christ; to whom, with thee and the Holy Ghost, be rendered honour and glory, for ever and ever. *Amen.*

For the two Sundays during the Holy Days of the Nativity.

O GOD! Creator of the world, Father of our Lord Jesus Christ, we lift up our hearts unto thee, we adore thy Majesty, we offer the humble sacrifice of praise and thanksgiving, more especially at this time, when so many of thy servants commemorate the nativity of their Redeemer.

Through thy great love towards mankind, thou didst send thine only Son into the world. Thou didst ordain that he should be born on earth; that there he should be subject to the infirmities of our nature; and that he should offer up, on the cross, for the salvation of men, the same body with which he had come into the world.

O LORD! we acknowledge, with joy and thanksgiving, that by his birth, and by his sacrifice, all who serve thee faithfully are raised from death into life, and made heirs of thy kingdom. We therefore magnify thy name, and adore thy mercy. Let all the angels extol thy glory and thy goodness! Let the sons of men proclaim thy great praise, and say, Glory be to God in the highest, on earth peace, good will towards men!

JESUS! Son of God! we bless thee that thou madest thyself man to redeem us; and we beseech thee to make us truly sensible of the efficacy of this redemption. Thou, who art the Son of the blessed God, the joy and glory of mankind, the Lamb of God which takest away the sins of the world, have mercy upon us. Thou, who wast upon earth, subject to infirmity as we are; who didst lay down thy life, and having taken it up again, art returned into the bosom and into the glory of thy Father in heaven, where thou sittest at his right hand, where the angels are subject unto thee, and where thou art preparing for us eternal habitations, favourably hear our prayers and receive our praises. Thou, who didst come to destroy the works of Satan, turn us from our iniquities. Thou, who wast born and didst live in lowliness, renouncing the pleasures and glory of the world, and submitting thyself even to the death of the cross, grant that we may despise the vanities and the deceitful riches of this mortal life, and may aspire only to that heavenly glory, and those everlasting treasures, which thou hast purchased for us. As thou hast so loved us, may we in like manner love thee, with all our heart, and may nothing ever separate us from thy love.

O GOD! we believe that thy dear Son was born to raise us to life eternal. Make us rightly to comprehend that, having this faith and this hope, we ought to purify ourselves, even as he is pure. Enable us worthily to celebrate thy praise, and to rejoice in the expectation of the glory to be revealed in us. And when this mighty Saviour shall again appear, with power and glory, for the sake of those who await his coming unto salvation, may we be made like unto him in thy kingdom, where he liveth, adored and glorified, through all eternity. *Amen.*

For the First Day of the Year.

O ETERNAL and Almighty God! we humble ourselves in thy presence, to dedicate unto thee the beginning of this year, by adoration, prayer and praise. We bow down before thy Supreme Majesty, and acknowledge, with gratitude, the manifold blessings which thou hast freely bestowed upon us, through the whole course of our lives. We thank thee, that having preserved us to the present time, thou hast permitted us to enter upon a new year.

THOU hast not ceased, O most gracious God! to vouchsafe to us the abundance of thy loving-kindness. But thou hast especially enriched us with thy spiritual blessings, by keeping in the midst of us the light of thy Gospel. Thou hast invited us to repentance, through thy mighty help, through thy great goodness, and through the warnings of thy word and of thy Spirit; and hast mercifully granted unto all of us favourable opportunities to grow in grace, and to attain unto salvation. Receive, O God! our praises and our thanksgivings; and, notwithstanding our unworthiness, for the love of Jesus Christ, take not away from us thy protection and thy favour.

O Lord! we would devote ourselves to thee, at the beginning of this year, desiring to employ it better than we have done the years which are past; and to this end, we ask thy grace and thy blessing.

And, since this day warns us, O merciful God! that our years pass away, give us grace seriously to consider that our end draweth nigh. Teach us so to discern the vanity of this life, that we may have an understanding heart; that we may aspire to that better life, when days, and months, and years, shall be counted no more forever; and that whilst we continue in the flesh, we may live no longer according to the desires thereof, but according to thy will. And grant, O God! that when our years shall come to an end, and the day of our death shall arrive, we may depart in thy peace, and in the hope of life everlasting. Favourably hear us, and receive our thanksgivings and supplications; through Jesus Christ our Lord. *Amen.*

For Palm Sunday.

BLESSED Lord! who of thy tender mercy towards mankind, didst offer thyself upon the cross, a sacrifice for sin; grant that, through thy grace, we may offer unto thee our souls and bodies a living sacrifice, holy and acceptable to thee, which is our reasonable service.

LORD Jesus! who didst enter into the city of Jerusalem amidst the acclamations and praises of the multitude and of thy disciples; who spread their garments in the way, and accompanied thee bearing in their hands branches of palm trees; give us grace to prepare thy way by all manner of good works, to bear before thee the fruits of righteousness, and to rejoice without ceasing in thy salvation. O Lord! who wast well pleased to be praised by the children in the temple, crying aloud, Hosannah to the Son of David! grant that, by imitating their innocence and simplicity, we may celebrate thy praises acceptably. And when thou shalt descend from heaven, at the last day, may we enter with thee into the heavenly Jerusalem, into the temple of thy glory, to praise thee and to bless thee forever. *Amen.*

For the Day of the Crucifixion.

ALMIGHTY God! we beseech thee to look favourably upon thy people, for whom our Lord Jesus Christ was willing to be delivered into the hands of wicked men, and to suffer death upon the cross. Grant that, as thy blessed Son shed his blood an atonement for our sins, we may thereby obtain pardon through thy mercy; and that thus we may draw near unto thee with a true heart, in full assurance of faith, and be enabled to serve thee, the living God; through the same Jesus Christ, our Lord.

O GRACIOUS and merciful God! who hast created all men, and hatest nothing which thou hast made; we offer unto thee our humble and fervent prayers for the ignorant and unbelieving. May it please thee especially, in thy great mercy, to look upon the children of Israel, once thy chosen people, now rejected because of unbelief, but not forever; and who still belong to thine election, for the sake of their fathers. Graciously hear the supplications of thy Church for their conversion, and remove from their hearts the veil of spiritual blindness and unbelief. O Lord Jesus! who didst come to save the lost sheep of the house of Israel; compassionate Redeemer! who didst pray for those who crucified thee; have pity on thine ancient people who still reject thee. Convert and bring back the remnant of Jacob; to the end that, looking upon him whom they pierced, all Israel, according to thy promises, may be saved.

ALMIGHTY God! we implore thy great mercy in favour of the heathen. Give them the light of thy Gospel, that forsaking their unbelief, they may know and serve thee, the living and true God, and Jesus Christ whom thou hast sent. Turn all Mahometans and Infidels from the error of their ways. O Lord Jesus Christ! the Great Shepherd of the flock, and Redeemer of the world, who didst lay down thy life for the salvation of all men; bring home thy sheep which are not as yet in thy fold; to the end that there may be but one fold and one Shepherd; and that the fulness of the nations having come into thy Church, every mouth may praise thee, and every tongue acknowledge thee to be Lord, to the glory of God, the Father.

FAVOURABLY hear us, O Lord! O Lamb of God! who takest away the sins of the world, have mercy upon us, and receive our supplications and praises; thou, who reignest with the Father and the Holy Ghost, One God, blessed forever. *Amen.*

For the Day of the Resurrection.

O GOD! we thank thee for the privilege of commemorating, this day, the fulfilment of the work of our redemption. We bless thee for thy mercy towards mankind, in yielding to the death of the cross thy well beloved Son, in whom was no sin; who was delivered up for our trangressions, and suffered for our iniquities; who gave his life an offering for sin, and who rose from the dead on the third day, as the great Shepherd of the flock.

CHRIST, our Passover, hath been sacrificed for us; Christ is risen from the dead; he hath conquered death, and liveth for ever and ever. The Stone which the builders rejected, hath become the head of the corner. This is the Lord's doing, and it is marvellous in our eyes. This is the day which the Lord hath made. Blessed be the God and Father of our Lord Jesus Christ, who, according to his abundant mercy, hath begotten us again unto a lively hope, by the resurrection of Jesus Christ from the dead; to an inheritance incorruptible and undefiled, and that fadeth not away, reserved in heaven for us. Accept, O Almighty God! the sacrifice of praise and thanksgiving which thy servants offer unto thee, on this day of the resurrection of their Redeemer.

O LORD! who hast opened unto us the way to a better life, by this resurrection of thy blessed Son; give us grace, that being risen with Christ, we may seek those things which are above, and not those which are on earth. May we live no more to ourselves, but to him who died and rose again for us; to the end that, in the day of his last coming, we may be partakers of the resurrection of the just; that our mortal bodies may put on immortality, and that we may be found worthy to obtain the happiness of the world to come, and life eternal; through the same Jesus Christ, who liveth and reigneth with thee, God blessed and glorified for ever. *Amen.*

For the Day of the Ascension.

O LORD God Almighty! we would now, especially, rejoice in thy holy presence, and bless thee for the ascension of Jesus Christ, our Saviour, who was taken up from earth into heaven. After thy Son had humbled himself, even to the death of the cross, thou didst highly exalt him, and hast given him a name which is above every name. Thou hast crowned him with glory and honour. Thou hast put all things under his feet, and hast made him to sit at the right hand of the Majesty on high.

O LORD Jesus Christ! thou hast entered into heaven. Prince of Peace! the everlasting gates have opened unto thee. Thy kingdom is an everlasting kingdom. Thou art the King of Glory. Thou art supreme in power, both in heaven and on earth. Thou art ascended to thy Father and our Father, to thy God and our God. Thou livest and reignest for ever and ever; and thou art able to save to the uttermost them who come unto God by thee. Thou hast entered into heaven as our forerunner. It is thy pleasure, that where thou art, there we should also be; and we believe that thou wilt come again, in like manner as thy Apostles saw thee ascend into heaven. We rejoice in thy triumph and thy glory. We beseech thee to make us partakers of the fruits of thine ascension, and to send down upon us from on high, thy Holy Spirit. Through thy death and ascension, thou hast opened heaven unto us. Suffer us not, by our ingratitude and our sins, to close it against us. Dispose us to seek the things which are above, where thou sittest at the right hand of God; and by holy meditations and fervent desires, to raise our affections towards heaven, thy dwelling-place.

O LORD Jesus Christ! who didst promise to thy disciples, before thine ascension, that thou wouldst be with them, even unto the end of the world; dwell with us according to thy promise, whilst we are in this body deprived of thy presence; to the end that, on the day of judgment, the day of thy last coming, we may hear with joy the voice of the Archangel; that when raised from the dead, we may be taken up to meet thee in the air; and may come to the heavenly Jerusalem, to the assembly of the first born, and of the just made perfect, to thee, the mediator of the new covenant, and to God, thy Father and our Father; to whom belong glory and blessing, for ever and ever. *Amen.*

For the Day of Pentecost.

ALMIGHTY God, Eternal Father! we praise thee and thank thee for all thy benefits, and, especially, for those which we commemorate at this time. We bless thee that thou hast redeemed us by thy Son, and that, after having exalted him to thy right hand, thou didst send down thy Holy Spirit upon the Apostles, and afterwards upon thy whole Church. May it please thee, O Lord! graciously to receive our thanksgivings and our praises for a gift so precious. Make us more and more sensible, of the efficacy of the blood which thy Son hath shed for us, and of the all-prevailing power of the Holy Spirit; to the end, that we may persevere in the holy calling wherewith thou hast honoured us, and that we may glorify thee all the days of our lives.

SPIRIT of Light and of Truth! lead us into all truth, enlighten our understandings, and dispel more and more the darkness thereof. Spirit of Prayer and of Supplication! teach us to pray as we ought, and create in us such holy desires as we cannot express. Spirit of Power! sustain us always by thine influence, be with us in temptations, direct us by thy grace without ceasing, and lead us continually unto well doing. Spirit of Holiness! sanctify our understandings and our hearts, purify our affections, and prepare us to do our duty, each in the vocation to which he is called. Spirit of Consolation! dwell with us always, comfort us in affliction, fill us at all times with joy unspeakable and full of glory. Spirit of Peace! give us gentle and charitable dispositions towards one another; give us that peace which the world can neither give nor take away.

O Holy and Divine Spirit! thou who didst descend upon the Apostles in cloven tongues, like as of fire, and didst bestow on them the gift of divers tongues; kindle in our hearts a heavenly flame; inspire us with such fervent zeal as will lead us to glorify thee, and to edify our neighbour, by all holy conversation, and pious works.

O God! cast us not away from thy presence, and take not thy Holy Spirit from us. Suffer us not to grieve or to quench this Holy Spirit. May he dwell continually in us, as in his Temple! May he guide us during our sojourn on earth, and may we rejoice without ceasing in his divine consolations! May we thus finish our course with joy! May our mortal bodies be one day quickened by the Spirit; and may we, at last, be accounted worthy to enter into thy glory, there to render eternally praise and honour to the Father, to the Son, and to the Holy Ghost. *Amen.*

For the Preparatory Service before Communion Day.

O OUR God, and our Saviour! we humble ourselves before thee, and thank thee for all thy mercies. We bless thee also, that thou dost graciously call us, though miserable sinners, to thy holy table, and to a participation in the benefits which Jesus Christ hath purchased for us, by his death and resurrection.

O LORD! sanctify us, we beseech thee, by thy Spirit; for we are of ourselves unworthy to appear at thy holy communion. Give us grace so to comprehend this holy and venerable sacrament, and, above all, thine exceeding love, that we may come to thy table with dispositions acceptable unto thee.

PRODUCE in us, O God! a deep conviction and a sincere repentance of our sins, a humble dependence on thy mercy, fervent gratitude for thine infinite love, and perfect confidence in the merits of thy Son, our only consolation in life and death. Grant unto us, O God, a firm resolution to serve thee according to thy will, and so to order our lives as becometh those who renew their baptismal vow, and again bind themselves to thy service. Give us also grace to love one another, even as thou hast loved us; and to forgive one another, in like manner as thou hast forgiven us.

LORD Jesus! supply in our hearts whatever is wanting to our preparation; preserve us from the danger of eating this bread and drinking this cup unworthily, and of thus rendering ourselves guilty of thy body and blood.

O LORD God! vouchsafe so to assist us by thy grace, that, now and at all times, we and thy whole church may commemorate, as we ought, the passion and love of thy Son. May Jesus Christ henceforth live in us; and may we live in him, walking in newness of life, even to the end of our days, to the glory of thy holy name, and to our eternal salvation; through the same Jesus Christ, our Lord. *Amen.*

A Prayer after Communion.

O OUR God, and our Father! Sovereign Lord and Ruler of all things, who art blessed in the heavens, and who art seated between the cherubim; thousands of thousands of angels continually worship before thee, celebrating thy glory and thy majesty, which fill the heavens and the earth. We praise thee, we magnify thy great mercy, and glorify thy name: for thy name is holy and glorious, greatly to be feared, and worthy to be exalted, now and forever, through Jesus Christ thy Son.

We offer unto thee, O Lord! our thanksgivings and our praises, with humility and joy, for as much as thou hast vouchsafed to receive us, miserable sinners, at thy table, and to number us among thy servants, and the heirs of thy kingdom. We beseech thee, through the merits of thy Son and faith in his blood, that we may be partakers of the fruits of his sacrifice, which we have this day commemorated. Grant that we may obtain, through thy mercy, remission of our sins, a sense of thy love, that peace which the world neither giveth nor taketh away, and an entrance into thine everlasting kingdom.

Send down upon us from heaven, thy Holy Spirit, to enlighten, to sanctify, to gladden our souls.

May we, through the same Spirit quickening us more and more, serve thee with a pure conscience, love one another with sincerity of heart, walk in innocence, and keep ourselves unspotted from the world.

So assist us, that whilst we are here in the body, we may keep the covenant which we have this day renewed, and may be faithful to thee even unto death. May this heavenly food which hath been provided for us at thy table, preserve and increase in us spiritual life, and destroy sin more and more in us. May we derive from this communion in the death of thy Son, victory over temptation, perseverance in faith, a sure defence against our spiritual enemies, and a continual growth in charity, humility and patience, that being enabled to lead a holy life, we may die the death of the righteous.

FINALLY, we beseech thee, O most gracious God! that as thou hast received us at this heavenly feast, prepared for us in thy church, we may be admitted, after our departure from this world, to the marriage feast of the Lamb, with all thy saints and all thine elect, in thy heavenly kingdom; where thou wilt be all in all, where we shall be conformed to thy glorious image, and shall eternally praise the Father, the Son, and the Holy Ghost. *Amen.*

SECTION SECOND.

Collects for Stated Occasions.

THESE MAY BE SUBSTITUTED FOR THE CORRESPONDING PRAYERS IN SEC. I., OR MAY BE USED IN THE AFTERNOON SERVICE.

For the Nativity.

O ALMIGHTY God! who didst give thine only Son, to take upon him our nature, and be born of a virgin; we implore thee to accept the praises which thy church offers unto thee, for this blessed nativity. Give us grace, that by a true faith, we may be partakers of the salvation which thy Son Jesus Christ brought into the world; and that, being ourselves regenerate and made thy children by adoption, we may serve thee in holiness and righteousness, all the days of our lives; through the same Jesus Christ, thy beloved Son. *Amen.*

For the Day of the Nativity.

O ALMIGHTY God! we thank thee that thou didst send thy Son, to be born of the Virgin, to the end, that becoming man, he might redeem us; and that thou wilt send him a second time from heaven to judge the world. Give us grace, that as we joyfully celebrate this day, the remembrance of the first coming of Jesus Christ, our Saviour, we may also appear before him, with gladness and a pure conscience, at the day of his second and last advent, when he will come in his glory, to judge the living and the dead. This we ask through the same Jesus Christ, thy Son, our Lord. *Amen.*

For the Last Day of the Year, and for New-Year's Day.

ALMIGHTY and most gracious God! since we are to close the year with this day, (*since we are this day beginning a new year,*) we thank thee for all the mercies vouchsafed to us during the whole course of our lives, and especially during the year now ending (*just closed.*) We offer unto thee, O Lord! the sacrifice of our praises, and we acknowledge, that through thy great goodness and help, we are enabled to pass our years in peace, although we have offended thee in various ways. Pardon, O merciful God! all who sincerely repent of their sins, and grant that, while our years are passing away, we may employ, in the work of our salvation, the time thou mayest vouchsafe unto us; pressing always towards the end of our heavenly calling, even that blessed eternity, which Jesus Christ thy Son, our Lord, hath prepared for us. *Amen.*

For the Day of the Crucifixion.

ALMIGHTY and everlasting God! who, of thy tender love towards mankind, didst not spare thine only Son, but didst deliver him up to death, that he might ransom us from our sins; give us grace, we beseech thee, so to keep in mind the sufferings and death of our Saviour, that, receiving this inestimable benefit with lively faith and sincere gratitude, we may obtain remission of all our sins. We pray thee also, that through the efficacy of his death, we may die unto sin, and live unto righteousness; that we may be led to love one another, and to follow the example of patience which our blessed Redeemer hath set before us; to the end that we may be made partakers of his resurrection; through the same Jesus Christ, our Lord. *Amen.*

For the Day of the Resurrection.

O GOD! who didst ordain that thine only Son should suffer death, should be buried and remain in the tomb until the third day; grant that we, who have been baptized into his death, may be likewise buried with him, by continually mortifying our corrupt affections. And as he rose from the dead, may we also rise in newness of life; so that, by death and the grave, we may pass to a joyful resurrection, through the merits of him who died for our offences, and rose again for our justification. *Amen.*

For the Day of the Ascension.

O ALMIGHTY God! since Jesus Christ, thine only Son, hath ascended into heaven, we beseech thee, to give us grace to ascend thither in mind and in heart. We pray thee, likewise, not to leave us comfortless, but that thou wouldst be pleased to send us thy Holy Spirit, to sanctify and to bless us, to lead and exalt us unto the place whither our Saviour Christ is gone before; who liveth and reigneth with thee and the Holy Ghost, One God, blessed forever. *Amen.*

For the Day of Pentecost.

O GOD! who didst send thy Holy Spirit, on the day of Pentecost, to thy faithful people; grant us the help of the same Spirit, to lead us into the way of truth and godliness, and to inspire us with sentiments of peace and charity; to the end that we may evermore rejoice in thy holy consolations; through the merits of Jesus Christ our Lord, who liveth and reigneth with thee, in the unity of the same Spirit, One God, blessed forever. *Amen.*

A Prayer before Communion.

ETERNAL and Almighty God! since we commemorate at this time the death of thy Son, in the celebration of the holy Supper, which he himself ordained as a pledge of his love and a memorial of his sufferings, to ransom us from our sins; we pray thee, favourably to look upon us, miserable sinners, who are unworthy to be partakers of these holy mysteries. Sanctify us, O Lord! that we may serve thee acceptably, in showing forth with faith and joy the death of our Saviour; and may glorify thee by holy and useful lives; through the same Jesus Christ. *Amen.*

A Prayer after Communion.

O ALMIGHTY God! we praise and thank thee, that in thine abundant mercy, thou didst deliver up thy Son to the death of the cross; and that we have this day had the consolation of commemorating that death, in the holy Supper. O God! we thank thee for a gift so precious. We extol thy mercy, and we pray to thee, that all of us, who have partaken of these holy mysteries, may profit by the sufferings of our Redeemer; and may obtain, through thy goodness, the pardon of our offences, the graces of thy Spirit, the comfort of thy love, the light of thy peace, and, after this life, the glory of thy kingdom. Hear us, we beseech thee, in the name and for the sake of our merciful Redeemer, Jesus Christ. *Amen.*

SECTION THIRD.

Occasional Prayers and Thanksgivings.

TO BE USED EITHER IN THE MORNING OR AFTERNOON SERVICES.

For a Person or Persons to be Ordained.

O GOD! who hast established a visible church upon earth, and hast ordained a holy ministry and sacraments therein; we pray to thee, at this time especially, for light and help to our pastors. May they admit to the sacred charge of preaching the Gospel, such persons only as are blameless in life, and pure, meek and fervent in spirit! May they be deeply sensible how solemn the duty is, to choose wisely and discreetly, those whom they shall receive into that holy ministry. More especially do we pray thee, at this time, to endue with thy Holy Spirit, and with heavenly gifts, our brother who is now to be ordained and dedicated to thy service. Sanctify him, to the end that, in purity of doctrine and holiness of life, he may serve thee faithfully, to the glory of thy holy name, and to the edification of thy church. Hear our prayer, O merciful Father! in the name and for the sake of our compassionate High Priest and adorable Redeemer, Jesus Christ. *Amen.*

For Pastors.

ALMIGHTY God! we pray thee for all the pastors of thy church. May they preach thy word with fidelity, firmness and humility. May they labour not in vain, to establish the indispensable obligation of the duties enjoined by our holy religion, and to make manifest their beauty and excellence. Enable them to set forth the motives which bind us to obey thee; the helps which are offered; and the rewards which await us. May they, as well by their example as by their preaching, prepare for thee a peculiar people, zealous of good works. Defend them, O Lord! under the shadow of thy wings; and guard them from the temptations of the world, and the devices of their spiritual enemies. Grant that they shun not to declare all the counsel of God; and that, having testified the Gospel of thy grace, they may finish their course with joy, and the ministry which they have received of the Lord Jesus. Hear us, O God! we beseech thee, for the sake of thy Son, our Saviour. *Amen.*

For Missionaries.

O ALMIGHTY God! who art the Father of all nations, and from whom cometh every good and perfect gift; who, in thy divine providence, hast appointed a ministry for thy church, with the command to teach all nations, baptizing them in the name of the Father, and of the Son, and of the Holy Ghost; we ask thy blessing on all missionaries throughout the world. Fill them, we pray thee, with zeal for thy church; and enable them to gather many lost sheep into the fold of the Redeemer. Endue them with innocence of life, and meekness of spirit. Grant them a strong faith, lively hopes, and above all, godly love. Give them grace to declare the whole counsel of God; to the glory of thy name; to the salvation of many, ready to perish; and to the advancement of thy Holy Church Universal. Hear us, we beseech thee, in the name and for the sake of the Lamb of God, who taketh away the sins of the world. *Amen.*

For Rain.

O GOD! heavenly Father! who, by thy Son, Jesus Christ, hast promised to those who seek thy kingdom and its righteousness, all things necessary for their bodily subsistence; we beseech thee to hear our supplications. Graciously send us rains and favourable seasons, that our hearts may be filled with joy, and that the earth may bring forth the fruits which are needful for us. O God! who didst provide for thy people, during forty years, in a barren and thirsty wilderness; command, we pray thee, the clouds to drop fatness through all thy heritage; and banish the drought from our borders. Overwhelm us not, merciful Father, with thy chastisements, but spare us, good Lord! and give us grace to praise and adore thee, through Jesus Christ, our Saviour. *Amen.*

Or this.

O GOD! heavenly Father! who, by thy Son Jesus Christ, hast promised to those who seek thy kingdom all things needful to their temporal comfort; grant, we beseech thee, that our land may be speedily refreshed with rain, to the relief of our necessities, and to thy glory; through our Lord and Saviour Jesus Christ. *Amen.*

For Fair Weather.

O LORD God Almighty! we acknowledge that, through our transgressions, we are justly exposed to thy displeasure. But we beseech thee to restrain thy righteous indignation, and to remember us in mercy. Withdraw from us the unusual rains wherewith we are visited. Vouchsafe to us favourable times for the growth and ingathering of the fruits of the earth, in their due season. Give us grace so to profit by thy chastisements, that we may love and fear thee more, through all the residue of our sojourn upon earth. Hear us, O merciful Father! for Christ's sake. *Amen.*

In Times of Dearth and Famine.

O GOD! heavenly Father! who givest the former and the latter rain; through whom the earth is fertile, the beasts of the field are nourished, and the fishes of the sea are multiplied; who holdest in thy hand the season appointed for harvest; amidst the abundance of all things, which thy loving-kindness has provided, we have neglected to serve thee, and thou dost now recall us to repentance and obedience by dearth and famine. We acknowledge, O God! that our sins have drawn upon us thine indignation. We cry unto thee, because the fountains of water fail. O Lord! grant in mercy, that the heavens may answer to the earth. Give unto all things their due increase, that we, receiving at thy bounteous hand the blessings which thou hast withheld, may devote them to the comfort of the destitute, to our own benefit, and to thy glory. These favours we humbly ask, O gracious Father! in the name of our compassionate Redeemer, Jesus Christ. *Amen.*

In Time of War.

O GOD! the Lord of Hosts! vengeance belongeth unto thee; thy power no creature can resist; but in wrath thou rememberest mercy. O gracious Father! restrain, we humbly beseech thee, the efforts of our enemies, and save us from the perils and evils of war. Inspire all who are high in authority over the nations, with dispositions to peace; and grant that the whole earth may become as one family. May glory to God and good will to men prevail upon earth, that we and all people may praise and serve thee, in all quietness. Hear, we beseech thee, our prayer, for the Redeemer's sake. *Amen.*

In Time of great Sickness and Mortality.

O LORD! we are consumed by thine anger, and by thy wrath are we troubled. Thou hast set our iniquities before thee, our secret sins in the light of thy countenance. Our days are passed in thy displeasure, and we spend our years as a tale that is told. Thou hast dealt justly with us, O Lord! in all things, for we have not obeyed thee. Thou hast seen that our wickedness was great, that the thoughts of our hearts were evil continually, and thou hast sent forth sickness and tribulation among us. The king of terrors is in the midst of us. O God! remember mercy, and withdraw from our land this awful scourge. O! say to this angel of death, it is enough, and of thy mercy spare us. But whatever the future may have in store for us, whether of good or of evil, give us grace to praise thy compassion with humility and fear, and to bless thy name for ever and ever; through Jesus Christ our Saviour. *Amen.*

For a Person expecting, or under, Sentence of Death.

WE implore thy mercy, O most gracious God! for the unhappy man in whose behalf our prayers are offered. O God! who desirest that the greatest of sinners should turn from his wickedness and live; we pray thee to seek this unfortunate prisoner, who, having forsaken thee, hath been surprised in his iniquities, and is about to suffer the punishment of the law, and to appear before thee.

O LORD Jesus! Saviour and Redeemer of men, who didst graciously hear the prayers of a malefactor crucified with thee; have pity on this convict, now cast down in thy holy and awful presence; give him repentance unto life; and grant that the punishment which awaits him may be sanctified to the salvation of his soul.

HEAR, O God! hear from heaven, thy dwelling-place, the prayers he may offer to thee in his distress. Favourably hear those who may intercede with thee, for him. If his body must suffer, may his spirit be saved in the day of the Lord. Although he may not escape the judgment of men, grant that he fall not under that awful condemnation, which destroyeth both soul and body.

These mercies, O Lord! we ask in the name, and for the sake of thy compassionate Son, Jesus Christ, our Redeemer. *Amen.*

For a Sick Person.

FAVOURABLY hear us, O Father of mercies! while we implore thy compassion in behalf of the sick person, for whom our prayers are desired. Visit *him* with thine infinite goodness, and sanctify unto *him* thy fatherly correction. May the sense of *his* danger strengthen *his* faith, and make *his* repentance the more sincere. Restore *him*, we humbly beseech thee, to the prayers of *his* family and of thy servants, who ask thy assistance, for the restoration of *his* health; and grant that the residue of *his* life may be devoted to *his* salvation, and to thy glory. But if it shall seem to thee good to order otherwise, give *him* grace to end *his* days in faith and hope, that *he* may dwell with thee in life everlasting; through Jesus Christ our Lord. *Amen.*

For a Sick Child.

ALMIGHTY and most merciful Father! in whose hands are the issues of life and death; look down, we beseech thee, in compassion upon the sick child, for whom our prayers are desired. If it be thy good pleasure, deliver *him* from *his* bodily sickness, prolong *his* days upon earth, enable *him* to live in thy fear and to thy glory, and visit *him* with thy salvation. But if it please thee, O gracious God! in thy wise providence, to take *his* soul at this time out of the world, receive *him*, we entreat thee, into those heavenly habitations, where the spirits of all who are in the Lord Jesus enjoy perpetual rest and felicity. Grant this, O Lord! for the love of thy Son, our Saviour, Jesus Christ. *Amen.*

For a Person under Affliction.

O MERCIFUL God and heavenly Father! who hast taught us, in thy holy word, that thou dost not willingly afflict the children of men; look with pity, we beseech thee, on the sorrows of thy *servant*, for whom our prayers are desired. In thy wisdom, thou hast visited *him* with trouble, and hast brought distress upon *him*. Remember *him*, O Lord! in mercy. Sanctify thy fatherly correction to *him*. Endue *his* soul with patience under *his* affliction, and with resignation to thy blessed will. Comfort *him* with a sense of thy goodness, and give *him* peace; through Jesus Christ our Lord. *Amen.*

For a Person, or Persons, at Sea, or going to Sea.

O ETERNAL God! who alone spreadest out the heavens, and rulest the raging of the sea; we commend to thy almighty protection, thy *servant*, for whose preservation on the great deep our prayers are desired. Guard *him*, we beseech thee, from the dangers of the sea, from sickness, from the violence of enemies, and from every evil to which *he* may be exposed. Conduct *him* in safety to the haven where *he* would be, with a grateful sense of thy mercies; through Jesus Christ our Lord. *Amen.*

THANKSGIVINGS.

For Rain.

O GOD! our heavenly Father! who, by thy providence, dost cause the former and the latter rain to descend upon the earth, that it may bring forth fruit for the use of man; we give thee humble thanks that it hath pleased thee favourably to hear our prayers; and in our great necessity, to send us rain for the dry and thirsty earth. For this thy mercy, we bless thee, O God! beseeching thee to give us grace to receive all thy gifts with thankfulness, and to use them according to thy will; through Jesus Christ our Lord. *Amen.*

For Fair Weather.

O LORD God! we return thee our thanks, that thou hast been graciously pleased to hear our supplications, and to withdraw from us the unusual rains, with which thou didst visit us. We thank thee that thou hast comforted us in our calamity, by a change so acceptable, and hast relieved our necessities. We praise thee, and we glorify thy holy name, for this testimony of thy fatherly love; desiring thy grace, always to remember thy goodness, and always to show forth our faithfulness, by obedience to thy holy will; through Jesus Christ our Lord. *Amen.*

For Abundance.

O MOST merciful Father! who hast graciously heard our prayers, and hast given us plenty instead of dearth; we give thee our humble thanks for this thy bounty. We beseech thee to continue thy loving-kindness unto us, that the earth may bring forth abundantly its fruits in their season.

We bless thee, O Lord! for these thy gifts, desiring to use them in thy fear, and in obedience to thy commandments; through Jesus Christ our Lord. *Amen.*

For Peace.

ALMIGHTY God! who art a tower of defence to all who put their trust in thee; we bless thee and give thee thanks, for our deliverance from the dangers which threatened us. O God! through whom men live in peace and concord; who only art able to calm the storms which disturb the tranquillity of our race; we return thee most humble thanks, that thou hast been pleased favourably to hear our supplications, and to give us peace. We praise thee, O Lord! for this thy mercy. Grant that the blessing thus graciously vouchsafed to us may be permanent. Above all, we beseech thee to give us that peace which the world cannot give, even thy peace; which passeth all understanding, and which keepeth our hearts and minds in Jesus Christ; in whose name, we offer up our sacrifice of praise and thanksgiving. *Amen.*

For Deliverance from great Sickness and Mortality.

O FATHER of Mercies! we humbly acknowledge that, through the multitude of our transgressions, and the hardness of our hearts, we might have been justly visited with all the judgments which thou hast denounced against sinners. But thou hast been graciously pleased, in thine infinite compassion, favourably to hear our prayers, and regard our imperfect humiliation. Thou hast withdrawn from us the grievous sickness which afflicted us. For this thy mercy, O Lord! we bless thee, and desire to present unto thee our bodies and our souls, a living sacrifice. Accept our thanksgivings; and enable us to live in love and fear of thee, and in obedience to thy commandments. Hear us, O compassionate Father! in the name and for the sake of thy Son, Jesus Christ. *Amen.*

For Recovery from Sickness.

O GOD of all compassion! receive our humble thanks for thy mercy vouchsafed to thy *servant*, who now desires to praise and bless thee for the restoration of *his* health. Thou knowest our frame, and rememberest that we are dust; and thou hast manifested towards *him* thy loving-kindness and tender mercies. We beseech thee, O gracious God! to impress *his* heart with a grateful sense of thy goodness; that *he* may, henceforth, love thee more and more purely, and serve thee more and more faithfully; so that, having lived acceptably to thee in this life, *he* may be partaker of thy glory in the life to come; through Jesus Christ our Lord. *Amen.*

For Recovery of a Sick Child.

O GOD! who art the giver of life, and the author of health unto all mankind; to thy providence we owe our preservation from day to day. It is of thy merciful goodness that the sick child, in whose behalf we approach thee, hath been graciously spared and restored. We unite with those whom thou hast ordained to be *his* guardians and friends, in returning our humble and hearty thanks for this manifestation of thy loving-kindness. May they be deeply sensible of thy great compassion; and may the child thou hast given back to them be a subject of thy grace, and an example of godliness and virtue, so long as *he* may live; through Jesus Christ our Lord. *Amen.*

For a Safe Return from Sea.

MOST gracious God! whose mercy is over all thy works, we praise thy holy name, that thou hast been pleased to conduct in safety, through the perils of the great deep, thy *servant*, in whose behalf we desire to return our thanks unto thee. Grant that *he* may be duly sensible of thy merciful providence towards *him:* and that *he* may also express *his* thankfulness by a holy trust in thee, and by a willing obedience to thy laws; through Jesus Christ our Lord. *Amen.*

For Deliverance in Time of Anxiety and Danger.

O ALMIGHTY God! thou hast been graciously pleased to preserve, amidst the anxiety and danger to which *he* hath been exposed, thy *servant*, in whose behalf we now desire to offer our praises unto thee. For this thy gracious deliverance, most merciful Father! we give thee humble thanks. And we beseech thee to grant that, through thy help, *he* may live according to thy holy will in this life, and may be partaker of everlasting glory, in the life to come; through Jesus Christ our Lord. *Amen.*

SECTION FOURTH.

Concluding Prayers.

For Purity of Heart and Life.

ALMIGHTY Father! who hast given thine only Son to die for our sins, and to rise again for our justification; cleanse us, we beseech thee, from the old leaven of malice, and of uncharitableness, that we may serve thee with singleness of heart and purity of life; through Jesus Christ our Lord. *Amen.*

For Divine Compassion and Blessing.

ALMIGHTY God! the fountain of all wisdom, who knowest our necessities before we ask, and our ignorance in asking; we beseech thee to have compassion on our infirmities; and those things which, for our unworthiness we dare not, and for our blindness we cannot ask, vouchsafe to give us; through the merits of thy Son, Jesus Christ, our Lord. *Amen.*

For Grace, Mercy, and Direction.

O GOD! the protector of all who trust in thee, without whom we have neither strength, nor faith, nor holiness of life; we beseech thee to increase thy grace in our hearts, and to multiply thy blessings upon us. Vouchsafe to be our ruler and our guide, that we may so pass through things temporal, as not to lose things eternal. Grant this, O heavenly Father! for the sake of our Lord Jesus Christ. *Amen.*

For Profitable Meditation, on the Works of Creation and Redemption.

O ALMIGHTY God! who didst create in six days, the heavens and the earth, and all that is therein, and didst rest on the seventh day; and hast created a new heaven and a new earth, by the ransom of the world, through Jesus Christ; give us grace so to meditate on the wonders of creation and redemption, that, knowing and adoring thee more and more, we may rejoice continually in thy marvellous works; and may enter one day into that eternal rest, which thou hast prepared for them that love thee; through Jesus Christ our Redeemer. *Amen.*

For Grace and Life.

O GOD! who desirest not the death of a sinner, but rather that he would turn from his wickedness and live; who despisest not the prayers and sighs of such as call upon thee; hearken unto us, and to all who confess their faults. Give thy grace unto those who are penitent. Turn us unto thee, that, forsaking our sins and living in newness of life, we may be acceptable in thy sight. Grant this, for the love of thy Son, Jesus Christ. *Amen.*

For Christian Love.

O GOD! who art the common Father of all mankind; and who hast taught us, that, although we speak with the tongues of men and of angels, and have all knowledge and all faith, and have not charity, we are nothing; we bless thee, that thou hast shown unto us this most excellent gift. We acknowledge, that, through our sinfulness and insufficiency, we fail continually in love to thee and to our fellow men. Endue us with grace to understand and believe, that charity suffereth long, and is kind; that charity envieth not, vaunteth not itself, is not puffed up, doth not behave itself unseemly; seeketh not her own, is not easily provoked, thinketh no evil, rejoiceth not in iniquity, but rejoiceth in the truth; beareth all things, hopeth all things, endureth all things. We beseech thee, O most compassionate Father! so to assist us in following the example of thy blessed Son, that we may experience in our hearts, and show forth in our lives, this grace; to the end that whether we live or die, we may glorify thee in love; through Jesus Christ our Lord. *Amen.*

For a Blessing on the Services of the Day.

ALMIGHTY God, our heavenly Father! it is of thy great goodness that we enjoy the precious advantages, of which so many are destitute. We have offended thee by our ingratitude, by our abuse of the privilege which thou hast vouchsafed to us, of knowing and serving thee; and thou mightest justly have removed the light of thy word from among us. O God! we adore thee for thy mercies; and we beseech thee, in thine infinite compassion, not to withdraw thy grace, but to sanctify us more and more, that we may serve thee with renewed zeal, all the days of our lives; through Jesus Christ our Lord. *Amen.*

Another.

ALMIGHTY God! bless, we beseech thee, the instructions of holy Scripture which we have heard this day, and all the services of thy sanctuary; that our hearts may be inclined to love and to fear thee; that we may serve thee faithfully, whilst we live; and that, having profited by the means and opportunities afforded for our salvation during this life, we may be received into the temple of thy glory, to praise thee forever, in the assembly of the saints; through Jesus Christ our Lord, in whose name we offer up our prayers. *Amen.*

Another.

O ALMIGHTY and merciful God! the source of all good, and the author of every perfect gift; we bless thee that we have been enabled, at this time, to meditate on the wholesome truths which thou hast revealed to us in thy word. Give us grace, we beseech thee, to profit by the instructions we have heard. So graft them in our hearts, that, being more and more strengthened in faith, we may serve thee with a pure conscience during the rest of our lives. Increase, O Lord! in our children, in our young people, and in all the members of this church, a knowledge of thee, and the fear of thy name. Grant, that being steadfast in obedience, and faithful even unto death, we may obtain, through thy mercy, that blessed and eternal life to which we are called; through Jesus Christ, thy Son, our Saviour. *Amen.*

Another.

ALMIGHTY God! who hast graciously promised to hear the supplications of those who ask in thy Son's name; we beseech thee, to accept the service and the prayers which we have now offered unto thee. May those things which we have faithfully asked, according to thy will, be effectually obtained, for the relief of our necessities, and to the advancement of thy glory; through Jesus Christ our Lord. *Amen.*

Another.

ALMIGHTY God! who hast given us grace, at this time, with one accord, to make our common supplications unto thee; and hast promised that when two or three are gathered together in thy name, thou wilt grant their requests; fulfil now, O Lord! the desires and petitions of thy servants, as may be most expedient for us, granting us in this world, knowledge of thy truth, and in the world to come, life everlasting; through Jesus Christ our Lord. *Amen.*

For the Afternoon.

[Taken from the Week Day Service, at page 36 ; to be used, on other occasions, with any of the Concluding Prayers.]

O ETERNAL and Almighty God! by whose gracious providence we have been preserved this day; protect us, we beseech thee, during the night. Preserve us from sin and danger; and give us grace to serve thee, at all times, in thankfulness. O Lord! we commit ourselves to thy care. Conduct us whilst awake; guard us whilst we sleep; so that, by day or by night, we may be always with thee; through Jesus Christ our Lord. *Amen.*

Another.

[Taken from the Week Day Service, at page 45; to be used as the preceding Prayer.]

O LORD! watch over us, and, through thy great mercy, defend our souls and bodies from all danger during the coming night; for the love of thine only Son, our Saviour, Jesus Christ. *Amen.*

SECTION FIFTH.

Family Prayers.

Morning Prayer.

O ALMIGHTY God! our Father and Preserver! we thank thee for thy watchful providence over us during the past night. Grant that, with a due sense of thy mercy, in bringing us safely to the beginning of this day, we may employ it acceptably to thee, by a willing obedience to thy commandment, of love to thee and to our neighbour. As thou sendest forth thy sun to shine upon the earth, a light to our paths; grant us thy Holy Spirit, to enlighten our understandings, and lead us into the ways of righteousness.

O God, our heavenly Father! be with us, we beseech thee, in all our employments; make it our concern to walk in thy fear, and to conform to thy will. Assist us to look to thy blessing on our labours, as the source of all our prosperity; and grant, that while we labour for things temporal, we neglect not things eternal.

O MERCIFUL Father! our Preserver and Protector! guard us both in our bodies and our souls; strengthen us against all the temptations of our spiritual enemies; and deliver us from every danger to which we may be exposed.

AND, for as much as it availeth nothing, to begin acceptably to thee, if we persevere not unto the end, vouchsafe, O gracious God! to receive us into thy holy keeping, not only this day, but through all the days of our lives. Increase in us, continually, thy saving grace, that we may enter into thy kingdom of eternal bliss and glory; through our Redeemer, Jesus Christ, the only Sun of Righteousness to our souls, to enlighten them by day and by night, forever.

AND, to the end that we may obtain these favours at thy hand, vouchsafe to us repentance and remission of our sins, according to thy gracious promises. Hear us, O Father! through our Lord Jesus Christ, in whose name we pray to thee, as he hath taught us, saying:

OUR Father, who art in heaven, hallowed be thy name; thy kingdom come; thy will be done on earth, as it is in heaven; give us this day our daily bread; and forgive us our trespasses, as we forgive those who trespass against us; and lead us not into temptation; but deliver us from evil: for thine is the kingdom, and the power, and the glory, for ever and ever. *Amen.*

Evening Prayer.

O LORD! our God and our Father! by whose gracious care we have been preserved during the past day; receive, we beseech thee, our evening sacrifice of praise and prayer. We bless thee, for our reason, and all other endowments and faculties of soul and body; for our health and friends; for food and raiment, and all other comforts and conveniences of life. But, above all, we bless thee, that thou hast vouchsafed to us a knowledge of thyself, and hast ordained us to be born into thy church. Suffer us not to be ungrateful for such precious favours. Grant that we may meditate thereon by day and by night, and that our gratitude may be manifest in our lives.

WE confess, O Lord God! our sins, negligences, and ignorances; and we humbly beseech thee, to give us repentance and forgiveness; and a firm trust in the sacrifice of our blessed Redeemer. And since, O Lord! we are, of ourselves, incapable of any good, grant us, for his sake, the aid of thy Holy Spirit.

O GOD! guard us, we beseech thee, this night; without thy care we cannot subsist for a single moment. May our minds be stayed on thee in perfect peace. May our strength, both of mind and body, be renewed by refreshing sleep; and may we awake on the morrow, full of thankfulness for thy mercies, and with holy purpose to live according to thy will.

We also beseech thee, O God! to dispose us, as we lie down in our beds, to think of that day when our bodies shall be laid in the grave, and our spirits shall appear before thee. Teach us to prepare for death, that it come not unawares; and may we always live, as knowing that we have to die.

Almighty and merciful God! continue, we pray thee, thy grace unto thy church; may it never be deprived of thy light. Bless the rulers of our country; and all pastors and teachers. Watch over our relatives, our friends, and our neighbours. Give knowledge of thy truth to all people; succour the poor; comfort the afflicted; and promote peace and good will among all men. We beseech thee to hear us, in the name of thy Son, who hath taught us to pray, saying:

Our Father, who art in heaven, hallowed be thy name; thy kingdom come; thy will be done on earth, as it is in heaven; give us this day our daily bread; and forgive us our trespasses, as we forgive those who trespass against us; and lead us not into temptation; but deliver us from evil: for thine is the kingdom, and the power, and the glory, for ever and ever. *Amen.*

PART FOURTH.

SECTION FIRST.

The Liturgy of Baptism and Confirmation.

BAPTISM.

The Minister shall commence the Service with the following Sentence.

OUR help is in the name of the Lord, who made heaven and earth. *Psalm cxxiv.*, 8.

The Minister shall then ask the Parents and Sponsors,

DO you offer *this child* to God, and to his holy church, requiring that *he* should be baptized?

They shall answer,

YES.

Then the Minister shall say,

THE Apostle St. Paul exhorteth, that prayers be made for all mankind: for this is good and acceptable in the sight of God; who will have all men to be saved, and to come unto the knowledge of the truth, through Jesus Christ; who gave himself a ransom for all.

SINCE then, we should pray for others, let us pray for *this child*, humbly, and with all our hearts.

ALMIGHTY God! Eternal Father! who hast promised us, through thy goodness, to be our God, and the God of our children, as thou wert the God of Abraham, and of his children; we pray thee, to receive *this child* into the covenant of thy mercy, and to make *him a partaker* of thy grace; to the end that, when *he* shall have come to the age of discretion, *he* may adore and serve thee only, and may live and die in thee; so that the baptism through which we receive *him* into thy holy church, may not have been administered to *him* in vain, but that *he* may be truly baptized into the death of thy Son, and into the newness of life acceptable to thee; through Jesus Christ our Lord. *Amen.*

Then shall the Minister say,

HEAR ye the Gospel which teacheth us the love of Christ, our Saviour, towards children.

St. Mark, x., 13–16,

AND they brought young children to him, that he should touch them: and his disciples rebuked those that brought them. But when Jesus saw it he was much displeased, and said unto them, Suffer the little children to come unto me, and forbid them not; for of such is the kingdom of God. Verily, I say unto you, whosoever shall not receive the kingdom of God as a little child, he shall not enter therein. And he took them up in his arms, put his hands upon them, and blessed them.

The Minister shall then say,

SINCE then, our Lord received and blessed, as you have just heard, the children who were brought unto him, we receive into his church *this child*, through baptism, and pray unto God to give *him* his blessing.

The Minister shall then say to the Parents and Sponsors,

YOU, who offer *this child* to be baptized, should consider, that God must be served in spirit and in truth. You promise, before God and this assembly, that you will be careful, you the *father and mother*, first and principally, and you also the sponsors, as far as by your duty you are bound and as necessity may require, to instruct *this child* in the Word of God, and in the Christian faith which we confess in the Apostles' Creed. You will teach *him* to worship the only true God, to call upon him in all *his* necessities, to ascribe glory to him for all good, and to acknowledge that all *his* righteousness is in Christ Jesus, and all *his* strength in the sanctification of the Holy Spirit. You will teach *him* to deny *himself*, to take up *his* cross, and to keep the commandments of God, the substance of which is, that we should love God with all our hearts, and our neighbour as ourselves. Finally, you will take care to exhort *this child*, and to reprove *him* when it shall be necessary, so that *he* may be brought up in the fear of the Lord, and according to his holy word; to the end that *his* whole life may be employed for the glory of God, and for the edification of *his* neighbour.

The Minister shall ask,

ARE these your promises?

The Parents and Sponsors shall answer,

YES.

The Minister shall then say,

THE Lord give you grace faithfully to perform these promises.

The Minister shall then baptize the child, naming him *and saying,*

N. N. I baptize thee in the name of the Father, and of the Son, and of the Holy Ghost. *Amen.*

After which, the Minister shall use the following Prayers and Benediction,

Let us pray.

O GOD! the Father, the Son, and the Holy Ghost! we beseech thee, to ratify in heaven what we have now done in thy name upon earth. Receive *this child* into the fold of the Good Shepherd; and bless *him* with all spiritual nurture; for our Redeemer's sake. *Amen.*

O HEAVENLY Father! who, by thy holy Prophet hast taught us that children are an heritage of the Lord; who also didst enjoin upon thy chosen people Israel, to teach their children thy statutes and ordinances; and who, through thine Apostle, St. Peter, hast assured us that the promise is unto us, and unto our children; we beseech thee to impress upon all parents, guardians and sponsors, and especially upon those who have at this time presented themselves before thee, a deep sense of the trust committed to them, in thy wise providence. Sanctify them through thy truth; and give them opportunity and disposition to perform their duties in faithfulness and love. And vouchsafe, O Father! to *this child*, and to all others who have been dedicated to thee in baptism, thy protecting care, and thy preventing grace. Give them meek and teachable dispositions, and a continual growth in the knowledge of thy truth as they advance in years; to the end that, through the means of grace provided in thy church on earth, they may at last be received into the church of the first born in heaven; through our Lord and Saviour, Jesus Christ. *Amen.*

THE grace of our Lord Jesus Christ, and the love of God, and the communion of the Holy Ghost, be with us all, evermore. *Amen.*

CONFIRMATION.

THE MANNER OF RECEIVING CATECHUMENS, BY CONFIRMATION OF THE BAPTISMAL VOW, TO A PARTICIPATION IN THE LORD'S SUPPER.

The Minister shall say to the Catechumens,

YOU have presented *yourselves* in the house of God this day, to witness a good profession of your faith. You were dedicated to God in baptism; and, being come to years of discretion, you desire, by your own act, openly to put on Christ. To this end,

Do you now ratify and confirm the engagements made in your behalf, at your baptism?

Do you renounce Satan and his works, the world and its pomps, the flesh and its sinful desires?

Do you promise, in dependence upon divine aid, to continue steadfast in the Christian faith, and to keep the commandments of God all the days of your life?

The Minister shall ask,

Are these your promises, before God and his Church?

They shall answer,

Yes.

The Minister shall then say,

God give you grace faithfully to perform these promises.

The Minister shall continue,

AFTER these promises, and in the hope that you may religiously fulfil them, you are received into the number of the faithful, to be *partakers* of the holy sacrament of the Supper.

And I call upon you, Christian brethren, who are here present, to witness the promises which *these young persons have* made; and I exhort you, to look upon *them* henceforth, as *partakers* with you of the same grace, and to offer up your prayers to God in *their* behalf.

An Exhortation, at the discretion of the Minister, is then addressed to the Catechumens; after which, they kneel, and the Minister offers the following Prayer.

Let us pray.

ALMIGHTY God! we bless thee, that thou hast been pleased to call us to a knowledge of thyself; and especially, that, having given grace unto *these persons* to be introduced into thy Church, through baptism, thou hast also graciously permitted *them* to arrive at years of discretion, and to ratify and confirm, this day, the vow of *their* baptism. We pray, that as *they have* now thus solemnly dedicated *themselves* to thee, and are to be admitted to the communion of the sacrament of the death of thy Son, thou wouldst ratify in heaven what we do in thy name, and in thy church on earth. Receive *them*, O Lord! bless *them*, and let thy grace be with *them*, now and for ever.

O GRACIOUS God! Father of mercy! grant that *they* may persevere constantly in the holy profession, upon which *they have* just entered, so that *they* may not only be *Christians* by birth and baptism, but may henceforth be such by knowledge and through choice. Since *they have* renounced Satan and his works, the world and its pomp, the flesh and its sinful desires, let the prince of darkness have no power over *them*; and grant that, henceforth, *their* faith may triumph over the world, the flesh and its wicked propensities. Holy Father! keep *them* in thy faith, and preserve *them* from evil. Sanctify *them* through thy truth: thy word is truth. Guard *them* from the corruptions of the world. Suffer not the instructions which *they have* received, and the promises which *they have* just made, to be ever blotted from *their* memory. Make *them* fruitful in knowledge and in faith, in holiness and in comfort, all the days of *their lives*. May *they* be better than *their* fathers; and, after having ministered in this world to the designs of thy providence, may *they* obtain from thy goodness eternal salvation.

O Lord! we pray unto thee for all the young people of this church. Bless the instructions which are given to them, preserve them from corruption, and sanctify them, so that our children may be one day ornaments in thy house, and heirs of thy kingdom.

Give grace to us all, the young and the old, the high and the low, to consider well what it is to be Christians; and to reflect continually what a vow, what promises, what a solemn profession, we have made at our baptism, as well as in the communion of the holy sacrament of the Supper.

Almighty God! hear us favourably, through Jesus Christ, who hath taught us thus to pray:

OUR Father, who art in heaven, hallowed be thy name; thy kingdom come; thy will be done on earth, as it is in heaven; give us this day our daily bread; and forgive us our trespasses, as we forgive those who trespass against us; and lead us not into temptation; but deliver us from evil: for thine is the kingdom, and the power, and the glory, for ever and ever. *Amen.*

The Minister shall conclude with the following Benediction.

THE grace of our Lord Jesus Christ, and the love of God, and the communion of the Holy Ghost, be with us all, evermore. *Amen.*

SECTION SECOND.

The Liturgy of Baptism for Adults.

The Minister shall commence the Service with the following Sentence:

OUR help is in the name of the Lord, who made heaven and earth. *Psalm cxxiv.*, 8.

The Minister shall then ask the Person *to be Baptized,*

DO you present *yourself* before God and his holy church, for baptism ?

He *shall answer,*

YES.

Then the Minister shall say,

HEAR, my brethren, how our Saviour instituted the holy sacrament of baptism, as it is recorded in the Gospels according to St. Matthew and St. Mark.

St. Matthew, xxviii. 18–20.

AND Jesus spake unto his disciples, saying, All power is given unto me in heaven and in earth. Go ye therefore, and teach all nations, baptizing them in the name of the Father, and of the Son, and of the Holy Ghost: teaching them to observe all things whatsoever I have commanded you.

St. Mark, xvi., 15, 16.

AND Jesus gave command to his disciples, saying, Go ye into all the world and preach the Gospel to every creature. He that believeth, and is baptized, shall be saved; but he that believeth not, shall be damned.

The Minister shall then say to the Person *to be Baptized,*

SINCE our Lord hath instituted this holy sacrament of baptism, and hath commanded, as you have just heard, that it should be administered to all who believe in him; and since you have signified your desire to receive the same, in testimony of your faith; we proceed, in conformity with holy Scripture, to administer it to you.

Then the Minister shall offer the following Prayer,

Let us pray.

ALMIGHTY God! Eternal Father! who hast promised us, through thy goodness, to be our God, and the God of all who believe in thee, and in Jesus Christ whom thou hast sent; we pray thee, to give thy Holy Spirit to thy *servant*, who here presents *himself* in thy presence. Receive *him*, O God! into the covenant of thy mercy, and make *him a partaker* of thy grace; to the end that *he* may know thee as *his* God; that *he* may adore and serve thee only, and may live and die in thee: so that this baptism, through which we receive *him* into thy holy church, may not be administered to *him* in vain; but that *he* may be truly baptized into the death of thy Son, and into newness of life acceptable unto thee; through Jesus Christ our Lord. *Amen.*

The Minister shall then say to the Person *to be Baptized,*

THESE are the holy engagements upon which you are about to enter, through baptism.

In the presence of God and this assembly, you profess, that you believe, and receive with all your heart, the Word of God; and that you desire to live and die in the Christian faith, which we confess in the Apostles' Creed. You profess to worship the only true God, and promise to call upon him in all your necessities, and to ascribe glory to him for all good. You profess to believe that all your righteousness is in Christ Jesus, and all your strength in the sanctification of the Holy Spirit. You promise, depending on Divine aid, to renounce Satan and his works, the world and its pomps, the flesh and its sinful desires; to deny *yourself*, to take up your cross, and to keep the commandments of God, the substance of which is, that we should love God with all our hearts, and our neighbour as ourselves. Finally, you promise, to watch and pray, that you may live in the fear of God, and according to his holy word; to the end that your whole life may be employed for the glory of God, and for the edification of your neighbour.

Then the Minister shall ask,

ARE these your professions and promises?

He shall answer,

YES.

The Minister shall then baptize the Person, *naming* him, *and saying,*

N. N. I baptize thee in the name of the Father, and of the Son, and of the Holy Ghost. *Amen.*

After which the Minister shall say to the Baptized Person,

YOU are now received into the number of the faithful, to be *a partaker* of the holy sacrament of the Supper.

MAY God give you grace to remember constantly the holy profession which you have embraced. May he ratify in heaven, that which we have done in his name, and in his church on earth; and give you his blessing now and evermore. *Amen.*

The Minister shall then say,

AND I call upon you, Christian brethren, who are here present, to witness the profession which *this person has* made in *his* baptism; and I exhort you to look upon *him* henceforth as *a partaker* with you of the same grace, and to offer up your prayers to God in *his* behalf.

The Person Baptized shall then kneel, and the Minister shall offer the following Prayer:

Let us pray.

O GRACIOUS God! Father of Mercy! we bless thee that thou hast been pleased to call us to a knowledge of thyself; and especially that thou hast given grace unto *this person* to enter into covenant with thee by baptism.

GRANT, O Merciful God! that *he* may constantly persevere in *his* holy profession. Since *he* has renounced Satan and his works, the world and its pomps, the flesh and its sinful desires, let the prince of darkness have no power over *him;* and grant that, henceforth, *his* faith may triumph over the world, the flesh and its wicked propensities. Holy Father! sanctify *him* through thy truth; and make *him* fruitful in knowledge and in faith, in holiness and in comfort, all the days of *his life;* and, after having ministered in this world to the designs of thy providence, may *he* obtain from thy goodness eternal salvation; through Jesus Christ our Lord. *Amen.*

THE grace of our Lord Jesus Christ, and the love of God, and the communion of the Holy Ghost, be with us all, evermore. *Amen.*

SECTION THIRD.

The Liturgy of the Holy Supper.

The Minister shall commence the Service with the following

INVOCATION.

Here the People rise.

IN the name of the Father, of the Son, and of the Holy Ghost.

Here, and at the end of the several Prayers, the People answer

AMEN.

Then the Minister shall say,

Let us pray.

O ETERNAL and Almighty God! whom all creatures praise and glorify as their Creator and Sovereign Lord; we beseech thee, as we are now assembled to partake of the holy Supper, which thy Son, our Saviour, Jesus Christ, commanded us to celebrate in remembrance of his death, that thou wouldst give us grace to perform this sacred duty, in a manner acceptable unto thee; through the same Jesus Christ. *Amen.*

Then the Minister shall say,

HEAR, my brethren, the institution of the Holy Supper, as it is related by St. Paul, in the eleventh chapter of the First Epistle to the Corinthians.

Here the People rise.

I HAVE received of the Lord, that which also I delivered unto you, that the Lord Jesus, the same night in which he was betrayed, took bread: and when he had given thanks, he brake it, and said, Take, eat: this is my body, which is broken for you: this do in remembrance of me. After the same manner also he took the cup, when he had supped, saying, This cup is the New Testament in my blood: this do ye, as oft as ye drink it, in remembrance of me. For as often as ye eat this bread, and drink this cup, ye do show the Lord's death till he come. Wherefore whosoever shall eat this bread, and drink this cup of the Lord, unworthily, shall be guilty of the body and blood of the Lord. But let a man examine himself, and so let him eat of that bread, and drink of that cup. For he that eateth and drinketh unworthily, eateth and drinketh condemnation to himself, not discerning the Lord's body.

The People being seated, the Minister shall continue,

YOU have now heard in what manner our Lord Jesus Christ instituted the Holy Supper; and with what purity and reverence it should be celebrated, even unto the end of the world, by all believers.

WE learn from holy Scripture, that none but true Christians should come thereunto, and that all such as are not of the number of the faithful are unworthy to be partakers thereof. To wit: the impious, the unbelieving, the profane, the blasphemous, those who live in strife and in hatred, impure, sensual and carnal men, drunkards, the unjust, those who withhold the goods of others, the covetous, the proud, evil speakers; and generally, all those in whom reigneth the love of the world and of its evil desires: upon all of whom, whilst they amend not, the anger of God resteth.

As for you, Christian brethren, who intend to come to this holy communion, you ought carefully to consider the solemnity of what you are about to do, lest you eat of this bread and drink of this cup unworthily. Judge ye yourselves, and ye shall not be judged of the Lord. And in all things, wherein ye know that ye have offended him, whether in word or in deed, in thought or in will, make confession thereof, with a humble reliance upon his mercy, and a true desire to live, henceforth, a righteous and godly life. Be ye, also, filled with sincere love towards your neighbour; if ye have done wrong to any, make reparation; and forgive ye one another, even as ye desire from God the forgiveness of your sins. If ye are thus minded, and if your consciences thus bear witness for you before God, who knoweth your hearts, ye may come to this holy table; and ye ought not to doubt that the Lord Jesus will there make you partakers of all the fruits of his passion and death.

BUT, above all things, ye must give at this time, your humble and hearty thanks to God, for the redemption of the world through Jesus Christ his Son; who did humble himself even to the death of the cross, for us miserable sinners, that he might make us children of God, and exalt us to everlasting life; and, to the end that we should always remember his exceeding great love, did institute this holy sacrament, to be unto us a pledge of his love, and a perpetual memorial of his death, to our great and endless comfort. To this merciful Redeemer, therefore, as well as to the Father and the Holy Spirit, let us now and always offer, as we are most bounden, our benedictions and our praises.

Then the Minister shall say,

Let us pray.

IT is meet and right, and our profitable duty, that we should, at all times and in all places, give thanks unto thee, O Lord, Holy Father, Everlasting God! through Jesus Christ our Lord; who for us was made very man, yet without sin; who died for our offences, and rose again for our justification; who by his death hath destroyed death, and by his resurrection hath given us eternal life; who hath ascended up on high, far above all heavens, where he ever liveth to make intercession for us; who also, according to his gracious promise, sent down upon the Apostles the Holy Spirit, to lead them into all truth, and to bestow upon them the gift of tongues, that they might preach the gospel unto all nations; whereby we have been brought out of darkness into light, and to a knowledge of thee; who also giveth us the Spirit of Adoption, and the blessed hope of pardon and peace, at the day of his glorious appearing:—

THEREFORE, with angels and archangels, and with all the company of heaven, we magnify thy glorious name; evermore praising thee, and saying, Holy, holy, holy, Lord God of Hosts, heaven and earth are full of thy glory, O God, most high!

AND since, O Lord! Jesus Christ, thy Son, did offer up himself as a sacrifice on the Cross, to redeem mankind, we beseech thee, in consideration of this sacrifice, that thou wouldst receive the supplications which we offer unto thy Divine Majesty, for the peace of the whole world, and for the salvation of all people.

WE pray thee to bless the Church Universal, with the spirit of truth, unity and concord; and to give grace to all who profess thy name, to follow with one consent thy holy word, and live in harmony and godly love.

VOUCHSAFE, O GOD! who art the source of all power, to bless and defend all Christian rulers and magistrates. So replenish them with the grace of thy Holy Spirit, that they may perform their duties with faithfulness, that religion may flourish, and righteousness advance among us.

SHED thy grace, O Sovereign Shepherd of our souls! upon all the ministers of thy church, that they may set forth the truth and power of thy holy word, both by their life and doctrine; that they may faithfully administer thy holy sacraments, and diligently watch over the flocks committed to their charge.

WE beseech thee, of thy goodness, to succour all persons who, during this transitory life, are in trouble, sorrow, need, sickness, or any other adversity.

FINALLY, O Lord! we pray thee for all this congregation here present, for all thy servants who desire to be partakers at thy table, and for all who show forth the death of their Saviour, and wait for his last and glorious coming; that through the communion in the death of thy Son, and through the efficacy of the precious blood which he shed upon the cross, we may be delivered from the wrath to come, and be found worthy to be received, with all thine elect, into the glory of thy kingdom.

HEAR us, O God, our Father! in the name of

Jesus Christ, our Saviour and Intercessor, who hath taught us to pray, saying:

OUR Father, who art in heaven, hallowed be thy name; thy kingdom come; thy will be done on earth, as it is in heaven; give us this day our daily bread; and forgive us our trespasses, as we forgive those who trespass against us; and lead us not into temptation; but deliver us from evil: for thine is the kingdom, and the power, and the glory, for ever and ever. *Amen.*

ALMIGHTY God! Father of our Lord Jesus Christ, before whom we now come to partake of the sacrament of the death of thy Son, graciously hear the confession of our sins. We acknowledge, O Lord! our unworthiness; we deplore the enormity and number of the sins which we have committed against thee; and we do not presume to come to thy holy sacrament, trusting in our own righteousness, but in thy great compassion. Have mercy upon us, O merciful Father! have mercy upon us. Pardon us, for the love of Jesus Christ; and give us grace this day, so to receive these sacred mysteries of bread and wine, that being united to thy holy Son through faith, we may live in him and he in us. We beseech thee to hear us, for the sake of the same Jesus Christ, our Lord. *Amen.*

The Minister shall then give the following invitation:

YE who truly repent of your sins, and rely wtth confidence on the mercy of God; who also are in sincere charity with all your neighbours; and are resolved, to conform your lives more and more to the commandments of God; draw near, and partake of the holy communion of the body and blood of our Lord.

The People shall then come to the Table.

The Minister shall then say,

Let us pray.

O ALMIGHTY God and Heavenly Father! who, through thy great mercy, didst deliver up thy Son to suffer death upon the cross for our redemption, we ascribe unto thee all glory and praise, through Jesus Christ our Lord; who offered up his own body as a sacrifice for the sins of the whole world, and commanded that a perpetual memorial of his death should be kept in his church, until his coming at the last day: For, the same night in which he was betrayed, he took bread;* and when he had given thanks to thee, O Eternal Father! he brake it, and gave it to his disciples, saying, Take, eat: this is my body, which is broken for you: this do in remembrance of me.† Likewise, after supper, he took the cup;‡ and when he had given thanks, he gave it to them, saying, Drink ye all of it; for this is my blood of the New Testament, which is shed for

* Here the Minister takes the bread in his hands.

† Here the Minister partakes of the bread, and gives bread to other Ministers, who may be at the table with him.

‡ Here he takes the cup.

many, for the remission of sins; this do ye, as oft as ye drink it, in remembrance of me.*

Then the Minister shall deliver the Communion to the People; and shall say,

In giving the Bread.

REMEMBER that Jesus Christ, thy Saviour, died for thee, and be thankful.

In giving the Cup.

REMEMBER that Jesus Christ, thy Saviour, shed his blood for thee, and be thankful.

The Communicants having returned to their Pews, a Hymn shall be sung; during which, offerings for the Poor may be received.

After which, the Minister shall say,

Let us pray.

HEAVENLY Father! we bless thee that thou hast been pleased so to favour us miserable sinners, as to receive us at the communion of thy Son, Jesus Christ, our Lord; who of God, is made unto us wisdom, and righteousness, sanctification and redemption. We bless thee, for having given him unto us as the bread of eternal life. Give us grace, never to forget these great benefits, but rather, having them graven upon the table of our hearts, to grow constantly in faith, and be fruitful in every good work, that our lives may be devoted to the advance-

* Here he drinks of the cup, and gives it to the other Ministers.

ment of thy glory, and to the edification of our neighbour; through the same Jesus Christ, who liveth and reigneth with thee, God blessed for ever and ever. *Amen.*

Then shall be sung the following Doxology; during which all stand.

GLORY be to God on high, and on earth peace, good will towards men. We praise thee, we bless thee, we worship thee, we glorify thee, we give thanks to thee for thy great glory, O Lord God, heavenly King, God the Father Almighty.

O Lord, the only begotten Son, Jesus Christ; O Lord God, Lamb of God, Son of the Father, who takest away the sins of the world, have mercy upon us. Thou, who takest away the sins of the world, have mercy upon us. Thou, who takest away the sins of the world, receive our prayer. Thou, who sittest at the right hand of God the Father, have mercy upon us.

For thou only art holy; thou only art the Lord; thou only, O Christ, with the Holy Ghost, art most high in the glory of God the Father. *Amen.*

The Minister shall then give the following

EXHORTATION TO THOSE WHO HAVE COMMUNED.

The People continue to stand.

I NOW exhort and beseech you, my beloved brethren, by the mercies of God, and by the love of the Lord Jesus, to consider well what we have just done, in the holy rite which we have celebrated.

We have solemnly acknowledged, by this act of thanksgiving, and by this public profession of our faith, that we have been ransomed from our sins and from eternal condemnation, by the death of Jesus Christ. We have testified that we are all brethren, and members of one body, and that we have a brotherly and sincere love towards each other. We have also promised to glorify God in our minds and bodies, by a life of holiness worthy of our vocation.

May God give us grace to remember well these promises, to perform them religiously, and to have the death of our beloved Redeemer so deeply graven in our hearts, that we may die daily, more and more, unto sin, and that we may walk in the ways of holiness all our lives, to the glory of God, and to our mutual edification. *Amen.*

The Minister shall then conclude the Service with one of the following

BENEDICTIONS.

NOW the God of peace, that brought again from the dead our Lord Jesus, that great Shepherd of the sheep, through the blood of the everlasting covenant, make you perfect in every good work to do his will, working in you that which is well pleasing in his sight, through Jesus Christ; to whom be glory for ever and ever. *Amen.* *Heb. xiii.*, 20, 21.

THE Lord bless you and keep you. The Lord make his face to shine upon you, and be gracious unto you. The Lord lift up his countenance upon you, and give you peace. *Amen. Numbers, vi.*, 24, 25, 26.

THE grace of our Lord Jesus Christ, and the love of God, and the communion of the Holy Ghost, be with us all evermore. *Amen. II. Cor., xiii.*, 14.

SECTION FOURTH.

Service for Occasions of Catechetical Instruction.

The Service may commence with a Canticle, Psalm, or Hymn, during which all stand.

Then the Minister shall say,

OUR help is in the name of the Lord, who made heaven and earth. *Psalm cxxiv.*, 8.

Here, and at the end of the following Prayer, the People answer,

AMEN.

Then the Minister shall say,

Let us pray.

O LORD, our God and our Father! since we are come together for the instruction of the young people of this church in the teachings of thy holy word; we give thee thanks, for having enlightened us by the knowledge of thy gospel, and for having made known unto us, through Jesus Christ, thy Son, the way that leadeth to eternal life.

We pray thee to bless these exercises, and to give to these young persons such docility, as may enable them to profit by our instructions. Thou hast caused them to be born into thy church; they have been dedicated to thee in baptism; thou art their Father and their God. O Lord! for the love of thy Son, who blessed the children that were brought unto him, and prayed for them; vouchsafe to bestow thy blessing on those whom we instruct, and to fill them betimes, with love and fear of thee. May the precepts of thy word not only enlighten their minds, but sanctify their hearts, and become the rule of their conduct; to the end that now, in the days of their youth, they may walk in the paths of piety, and thus attain to the glory of the kingdom of heaven.

Give thy grace to fathers and mothers, to bring up their children under thy guidance. Bless all the families of this church. Sanctify the young people. Grant the knowledge and the fear of thee to persons of every age and condition; so that all of us may increase in faith and piety, as we advance in years. Make us all to be as children in innocence and humility; grant that the knowledge which thou hast given us, and the glory which we look for, may lead us to love thee, and to live in those good works which thou hast ordained that we should walk in. Favourably hear us, O Almighty God! for the love of Jesus Christ, who hath taught us thus to pray, saying:

OUR Father, who art in heaven, hallowed be thy name; thy kingdom come; thy will be done on earth, as it is in heaven; give us this day our daily bread; and forgive us our trespasses, as we forgive those who trespass against us; and lead us not into temptation; but deliver us from evil: for thine is the kingdom, and the power, and the glory, for ever and ever. *Amen.*

Or this.

O LORD! as we are now about to instruct the youth of this church, we implore thee to shed thy blessing on our labours, and to give unto these young persons the docility requisite to profit thereby. Since they have been consecrated to thee from their infancy; and thou art their Father and their God, vouchsafe to take them under thy protection, to sanctify them by thy Spirit, and to fill them with the love and the fear of thee; to the end, that they may hereafter be among the truly faithful in thy church, and among the ever blessed in thy kingdom; through the mercy and love of Jesus Christ our Lord. *Amen.*

OUR Father, who art in heaven, hallowed be thy name; thy kingdom come; thy will be done on earth, as it is in heaven; give us this day our daily bread; and forgive us our trespasses, as we forgive those who trespass against us; and lead us not into temptation; but deliver us from evil: for thine is the kingdom, and the power, and the glory, for ever and ever. *Amen.*

Then the Recitation of the Children shall follow.

After which, a Benediction.

THE grace of our Lord Jesus Christ, and the love of God, and the communion of the Holy Ghost, be with us all evermore. *Amen. II. Cor., xiii.,* 14.

SECTION FIFTH.

The Liturgy of Marriage.

The Minister shall commence the Service with the following Sentence.

OUR help is in the name of the Lord, who made heaven and earth. *Psalm cxxiv.*, 8.

Then the Minister shall say,

GOD our Father, having created heaven and earth, and all that in them is, made man in his own image, and gave him dominion over the beasts of the field, over the fish of the sea, over the fowl of the air, and over every living thing that moveth upon the earth. And after he had created man, God said, It is not good that the man should be alone: I will make him a help meet for him. And the Lord God made woman, bone of his bone, and flesh of his flesh, signifying thereby that they two were one.

WHEREFORE, our blessed Lord, when the Pharisees came unto him, tempting him, and saying unto him, Is it lawful for a man to put away his wife for every cause? answered and said unto them:—Have ye not read, that he which made them at the beginning, made them male and female, and said, For this cause shall a man leave father and mother, and shall cleave to his wife: and they twain shall be one flesh? So then they are no more twain, but one flesh. What therefore God hath joined together, let not man put asunder.

AND the Apostle St. Paul, who commendeth marriage as honourable in all, saith:—So ought men to love their wives as their own bodies; he that loveth his wife, loveth himself. For no man ever yet hated his own flesh, but nourisheth and cherisheth it. Likewise, let the wife see that she reverence her husband, and submit herself unto her own husband, as it is fit in the Lord.

SEEING, then, that this holy covenant of Matrimony, which God hath ordained, is of such authority and obligation; it is not to be entered into unadvisedly or lightly, but reverently, discreetly, and soberly, in the fear of God, and with holy purpose to live therein in all purity, according to his will.

Addressing the Persons to be Married, the Minister shall say,

M. and N.—ARE you willing to enter into the holy state of Matrimony, which God hath instituted, to live together therein, according to his commandments? And do you desire to make known here, before God and this company, (*or congregation,*) this your purpose?

They shall answer,

YES.

Then the Minister shall say,

GOD confirm and bless your purpose.

Let us pray.

O ETERNAL God! the author of every good and perfect gift, we thank thee that thou hast ordained the institution of marriage; and we beseech thee to send thy blessing upon these thy servants, who are now about to be joined together in this holy estate. Give them a just sense of thy presence, and of the obligation of the covenant they are about to make; to the end that this solemn service may have a wholesome influence upon their affections and conduct throughout life, to the glory of thy name; through Jesus Christ our Lord. *Amen.*

The Minister shall then say to the Man,

M. Do you acknowledge here, before God and this company, (*or congregation,*) that you have agreed to take, and that you now take, N. for your wife? Do you promise to love, honour and protect her;

to maintain, comfort and cherish her, in health and in sickness, in joy and in sorrow, in prosperity and in adversity; to lead a holy life with her, being faithful unto her in all things; as is the duty of a good husband, according to the word of God?

Answer.—YES.

The Minister shall then say unto the Woman,

N. Do you also acknowledge here, before God and this company, (*or congregation,*) that you have agreed to take, and that you now take, M. for your husband! Do you promise to love, honour and obey him; to comfort and cherish him, in health and in sickness, in joy and in sorrow, in prosperity and in adversity; to lead a holy life with him, being faithful unto him in all things; as is the duty of a good wife, according to the word of God?

Answer.—YES.

[*To be used, or not, at the discretion of the Parties.*

IN testimony, that you M. and N. do advisedly and solemnly ratify all that hath been declared and promised by you, do thou M. acknowledge and endow this woman as thy wife, by delivering unto her a ring, in token of thy faith; and do thou N. in like manner receive the same, as a pledge of his faith, and as a witness of thy vows.

Then the Man delivers to the Woman a ring, placing it upon the fourth finger of her left hand.]

Then shall the Minister join their right hands together, and say,

YOU are now Man and Wife.

THOSE whom God hath joined together, let not man put asunder.

Then the Minister shall say,

LET us pray to God our Father, for his blessing upon these his servants.

O ALMIGHTY, all-merciful, and all-wise God! we pray thee in behalf of these persons, who have entered into the holy estate of marriage, that thou wouldst vouchsafe to them thy Holy Spirit. Send down thy blessing upon these thy servants, whom we bless in thy name. Enable them to observe surely, and to perform faithfully, the vows and covenant between them made; and, mutually edifying each other, to live together in purity, concord and piety. Give them grace to reverence and serve thee, and to contribute to the advancement of thy glory, the honour of the gospel, and the welfare of thy church. Favourably hear us, O Father of Mercy! in the name and for the sake of thy dear Son. *Amen.*

Then the Minister shall add this Benediction,

GOD, the Father, the Son, and the Holy Ghost, bless, preserve and guide you. May you be filled with all spiritual benediction, and so live together in this life, that, in the world to come, you may have life everlasting. *Amen.*

SECTION SIXTH.

Service for the Burial of the Dead.

TAKEN FROM THE BOOK OF COMMON PRAYER OF THE PROTESTANT EPISCOPAL CHURCH OF U. S.

THE MINISTER MAY READ THE WHOLE, OR SUCH PART OF THIS SERVICE AS HE MAY THINK FIT.

The Minister, meeting the Corpse at the entrance of the Church, and going before it, either into the Church, or towards the Grave, shall say,

I AM the resurrection and the life, saith the Lord: he that believeth in me, though he were dead, yet shall he live: And whosoever liveth and believeth in me, shall never die. *St. John, xi.*, 25, 26.

I KNOW that my Redeemer liveth, and that he shall stand at the latter day upon the earth. And though after my skin worms destroy this body, yet in my flesh shall I see God: whom I shall see for myself, and mine eyes shall behold, and not another. *Job xix.*, 25–27.

WE brought nothing into this world, and it is certain we can carry nothing out. The Lord gave, and the Lord hath taken away; blessed be the name of the Lord. *I. Tim., vi.* 7; *Job i.*, 21.

After they are come into the Church, shall be said or sung the following Anthem, taken from the xxxixth and xcth Psalms.

During which the People stand.

From Psalm xxxix.

LORD, let me know my end, and the number of my days; that I may be certified how long I have to live.

Behold, thou hast made my days, as it were a span long, and mine age is even as nothing in respect of thee; and verily every man living is altogether vanity.

For man walketh in a vain shadow, and disquieteth himself in vain; he heapeth up riches, and cannot tell who shall gather them.

And now, Lord! what is my hope? Truly my hope is even in thee.

Deliver me from all mine offences; and make me not a rebuke unto the foolish.

When thou with rebukes dost chasten man for sin, thou makest his beauty to consume away, like as it were a moth fretting a garment: every man therefore is but vanity.

Hear my prayer, O Lord! and with thine ears

consider my calling; hold not thy peace at my tears:

For I am a stranger with thee, and a sojourner, as all my fathers were.

O spare me a little, that I may recover my strength, before I go hence, and be no more seen.

From Psalm xc.

LORD, thou hast been our refuge, from one generation to another.

Before the mountains were brought forth, or ever the earth and the world were made, thou art God from everlasting, and world without end.

Thou turnest man to destruction; again thou sayest, Come again, ye children of men.

For a thousand years in thy sight are but as yesterday; seeing that is past as a watch in the night.

As soon as thou scatterest them, they are even as a sleep; and fade away suddenly like the grass.

In the morning it is green, and groweth up; but in the evening it is cut down, dried up, and withered.

For we consume away, in thy displeasure; and are afraid at thy wrathful indignation.

Thou hast set our misdeeds before thee; and our secret sins in the light of thy countenance.

For when thou art angry, all our days are gone; we bring our years to an end, as it were a tale that is told.

The days of our age are threescore years and ten;

and though men be so strong that they come to fourscore years, yet is their strength then but labour and sorrow; so soon passeth it away, and we are gone.

So teach us to number our days, that we may apply our hearts unto wisdom.

Glory be to the Father, and to the Son, and to the Holy Ghost; as it was in the beginning, is now, and ever shall be, world without end. *Amen.*

Then shall follow the Lesson, taken out of the fifteenth Chapter of the First Epistle of St. Paul to the Corinthians,

NOW is Christ risen from the dead, and become the first fruits of them that slept. For since by man came death, by man came also the resurrection of the dead. For as in Adam all die, even so in Christ shall all be made alive. But every man in his own order: Christ the first fruits; afterward, they that are Christ's at his coming. Then cometh the end, when he shall have delivered up the kingdom to God, even the Father; when he shall have put down all rule, and all authority, and power. For he must reign, till he hath put all enemies under his feet. The last enemy that shall be destroyed is death. For he hath put all things under his feet. But when he saith, all things are put under him, it is manifest that he is excepted, which did put all things under him. And when all things shall be subdued unto him, then shall the Son also himself be subject unto Him that put all things under him, that God may be all in all. Else what shall they do, which are baptized for the dead, if the dead rise not at all? Why are they then baptized for the dead? And why stand we in jeopardy every hour? I protest by your rejoicing, which I have in Christ Jesus our Lord, I die daily. If after the manner of men I have fought with beasts at Ephesus, what advantageth it me, if the dead rise not? Let us eat and drink; for to-morrow we die. Be not deceived: evil communications corrupt good manners. Awake to righteousness, and sin not; for some have not the knowledge of God. I speak this to your shame. But some man will say, How are the dead raised up? and with what body do they come? Thou fool! that, which thou sowest, is not quickened, except it die. And that which thou sowest, thou sowest not that body that shall be, but bare grain, it may chance of wheat, or of some other grain. But God giveth it a body as it hath pleased him; and to every seed, his own body. All flesh is not the same flesh; but there is one kind of flesh of men, another flesh of beasts, another of fishes, and another of birds. There are also celestial bodies, and bodies terrestrial; but the glory of the celestial is one, and the glory of the terrestrial is another. There is one glory of the sun, and another glory of the moon, and another glory of the stars; for one star differeth from another star in glory. So also is the resurrection of the dead. It is sown in corruption; it is raised in incorruption: it is sown in dishonour; it is raised in glory: it is sown in weakness; it is raised in power: it is sown a natural body; it is raised a spiritual body. There is a natural body, and there is a spiritual body. And so it is written, The first man Adam was made a living soul; the last Adam was made a quickening spirit. Howbeit, that was not first which is spiritual, but that which is natural; and afterward that which is spiritual. The first man is of the earth, earthy: the second man the Lord from heaven. As is the earthy, such are they that are earthy; and as is the heavenly, such are they also that are heavenly. And as we have borne the image of the earthy, we shall also bear the image of the heavenly. Now this I say, brethren, that flesh and blood cannot inherit the kingdom of God; neither doth corruption inherit incorruption. Behold, I show you a mystery. We shall not all sleep, but we shall be changed, in a moment, in the twinkling of an eye, at the last trump: for the trumpet shall sound, and the dead shall be raised incorruptible, and we shall be changed. For this corruptible must put on incorruption, and this mortal must put on immortality. So when this corruptible shall have put on incorruption, and this mortal shall have put on immortality, then shall be brought to pass the saying that is written, Death is swallowed up in victory. O death, where is thy sting? O grave, where is thy victory? The sting of death is sin, and the strength of sin is the law. But thanks be to God, which giveth us the victory, through our Lord Jesus Christ.

Therefore, my beloved brethren, be ye steadfast, unmoveable, always abounding in the work of the Lord; forasmuch as ye know that your labour is not in vain in the Lord.

Then may be sung a Hymn.

Then, in the Church, or at the Grave, shall be said,

MAN, that is born of a woman, hath but a short time to live, and is full of misery. He cometh up, and is cut down, like a flower; he fleeth as it were a shadow, and never continueth in one stay.

In the midst of life we are in death: of whom may we seek for succour, but of thee, O Lord! who for our sins art justly displeased?

Yet, O Lord God most holy! O Lord most mighty! O holy and most merciful Saviour! deliver us not into the bitter pains of eternal death.

Thou knowest, Lord! the secrets of our hearts; shut not thy merciful ears to our prayer; but spare us, Lord most holy! O God most mighty! O holy and merciful Saviour! thou most worthy Judge eternal, suffer us not, at our last hour, for any pains of death, to fall from thee.

Then, while the earth shall be cast upon the Body, by some standing by, the Minister shall say,

FORASMUCH as it hath pleased Almighty God, in his wise providence, to take out of this world the soul of our deceased *brother*, we therefore commit *his* body to the ground; earth to earth, ashes to ashes, dust to dust; looking for the general resurrection in the last day, and the life of the world to come, through our Lord Jesus Christ; at whose second coming in glorious majesty to judge the world, the earth and the sea shall give up their dead; and the corruptible bodies of those who sleep in him shall be changed, and made like unto his own glorious body; according to the mighty working, whereby he is able to subdue all things unto himself.

Then shall be said, or sung,

I HEARD a voice from heaven, saying unto me, Write, From henceforth, blessed are the dead who die in the Lord; even so, saith the Spirit, for they rest from their labours. *Rev. xiv.*, 13.

Then the Minister shall say the Lord's Prayer, and one or both the following Prayers, at his discretion, and conclude with the Benediction.

OUR Father, who art in heaven, hallowed be thy name; thy kingdom come; thy will be done on earth, as it is in heaven; give us this day our daily bread; and forgive us our trespasses, as we forgive those who trespass against us; and lead us not into temptation; but deliver us from evil: for thine is the kingdom, and the power, and the glory, for ever and ever. *Amen.*

ALMIGHTY God! with whom do live the spirits of those who depart hence in the Lord; and with whom the souls of the faithful, after they are delivered from the burden of the flesh, are in joy and felicity; we give thee hearty thanks for the good examples of all those thy servants, who, having finished their course in faith, do now rest from their labours. And we beseech thee, that we, with all those who are departed in the true faith of thy holy name, may have our perfect consummation and bliss, both in body and soul, in thy eternal and everlasting glory, through Jesus Christ our Lord. *Amen.*

O MERCIFUL God! the Father of our Lord Jesus Christ, who is the resurrection and the life; in whom whosoever believeth, shall live, though he die; and whosoever liveth and believeth in him, shall not die eternally; who also hath taught us, by his holy Apostle St. Paul, not to be sorry, as men without hope, for those who sleep in him; we humbly beseech thee, O Father! to raise us from the death of sin unto the life of righteousness; that, when we shall depart this life, we may rest in him; and that, at the general resurrection in the last day, we may be found acceptable in thy sight; and receive that blessing, which thy well-beloved Son shall then pronounce on all who love and fear thee, saying, Come, ye blessed children of my Father, receive the kingdom prepared for you, from the beginning of the world. Grant this, we beseech thee, O merciful Father! through Jesus Christ, our Mediator and Redeemer. *Amen.*

THE grace of our Lord Jesus Christ, and the love of God, and the communion of the Holy Ghost, be with us all evermore. *Amen.*

PART FIFTH.

Canticles for the Ordinary Service.

First Canticle.

O COME! let us sing unto the Lord; let us heartily rejoice in the Rock of our salvation.

Let us come before his presence with thanksgiving; and show ourselves glad in him with psalms.

O come! let us worship and bow down; let us kneel before the Lord our Maker.

For he is the Lord, our God, and we are the people of his pasture, and the sheep of his hand.

Manifold, O God! are thy wondrous and bounteous works: they are more than can be numbered.

In thee we live, and move, and have our being. The testimonies of thy loving kindness are ever about us.

Thou hast sent thine only Son into the world, to be a propitiation for our sins.

For all these things we bless thee, and we magnify thy glorious name; saying with the angels and all the heavenly host,

Holy, Holy, Holy, Lord God of hosts! Heaven and earth are full of thy glory, O God! most high.

Let our mouths show forth thy praise for ever.

Let all that hath breath, bless thee for ever and ever.

Glory be to the Father, and to the Son, and to the Holy Ghost; as it was in the beginning, is now, and ever shall be, world without end. *Amen.*

Second Canticle.

O YE righteous! sing unto the Lord with joy; for it becometh well the just to be thankful.

Praise the Lord, sing unto him a new song: for all his works are done in truth.

All the earth is full of the goodness of the Lord: let all the inhabitants of the world stand in awe of him.

I will wash my hands in innocency; so will I compass thine altar, O Lord!

And with the voice of thanksgiving, tell of all thy wondrous works.

My God! I love the habitation of thy house, and the place where thine honour dwelleth.

Cause us to hear thy loving kindness in the morning; for in thee do we trust.

Cause us to know the way wherein we should walk; for we lift up our souls unto thee.

Let us bless the Lord, who crowneth us day by day with his benefits.

Giving thanks unto the Father, which hath made us meet to be partakers of the inheritance of the saints in light.

Who hath delivered us from the power of darkness, and hath translated us into the kingdom of his dear Son.

Glory be, &c.

Third Canticle.

PRAISE ye the Lord, call upon his name; make known his deeds among the people.

Sing unto him; sing psalms unto him; tell ye of all his wondrous works.

Rejoice ye in his holy name; let the hearts of those rejoice who seek the Lord.

Seek the Lord and his strength; seek his face evermore; remember his marvellous works.

Great is our Lord and great is his power: his wisdom is infinite.

Sing unto the Lord with thanksgiving, answering one unto another; sing psalms unto our God.

Praise the Lord, O Jerusalem! Praise thy God, O Zion.

He strengtheneth the bars of thy gates, and blesseth thy children within thee.

He showeth his word unto Jacob, his statutes and ordinances unto Israel:

He hath not dealt so with any nation.

He so loved the world, that he gave his only Son, that whosoever believeth in him should not perish, but have everlasting life.

What shall we render unto the Lord, for all his benefits towards us.

We will receive the cup of salvation, and call upon the name of the Lord.

Glory be, &c.

Fourth Canticle.

WE will extol thee, O God, our King! and we will bless thy name for ever and ever.

Great is the Lord, and greatly to be praised; his greatness is unsearchable.

One generation shall praise thy works unto another.

The Lord is gracious and full of compassion, slow to anger and of great mercy.

The Lord is good to all; his tender mercies are over all his works.

All thy works shall praise thee, O Lord! and thy saints shall bless thee;

They shall speak of the glory of thy kingdom, and talk of thy power.

Thy kingdom is an everlasting kingdom, and thy dominion endureth throughout all ages.

The Lord upholdeth all those who fall; and raiseth up all who are bowed down.

The eyes of all wait upon thee, and thou givest them their meat in due season.

Thou openest thine hand, and satisfiest the desire of every living thing.

The Lord is righteous in all his ways, and holy in all his works.

The Lord is nigh unto all them that call upon him; unto all that call upon him in truth.

He fulfilleth the desire of those who fear him; he heareth their cry and saveth them.

The Lord preserveth all those who love him; but all the wicked will he destroy.

Our mouth shall speak the praise of the Lord, and we will bless his holy name for ever and ever.

Glory be, &c.

Fifth Canticle.

O GOD! we praise thee with our whole heart; we worship before thee in thy holy temple.

We praise thy name for thy loving kindness and thy truth; we rejoice in thy salvation.

Thou hast sent thy Son to fulfil the promises made unto the fathers;

To the end that the Gentiles might praise thee for thy mercy.

Wherefore, we will praise thee among the nations, and sing unto thy name.

Rejoice, O ye Gentiles! with his people.

O! praise the Lord, all ye nations, and celebrate him all ye people;

Ye who in time past, were not his people, but are now the people of God;

Ye, who in time past had not obtained mercy, but now have obtained mercy.

O! the depth of the riches of the wisdom and knowledge of God!

How unsearchable are his judgments, and his ways past finding out!

Who hath known the mind of the Lord, and who hath been his counsellor?

For of him, and through him, and to him, are all things, to whom be glory for ever.

Glory be, &c.

Sixth Canticle.

O! LET us be joyful in the Lord our God. Let us serve the Lord with gladness, and come before his presence with a song.

Know ye that the Lord is God; it is he who hath made us, and not we ourselves; we are his people, and the sheep of his pasture.

Enter into his gates with thanksgiving, and into

his courts with praise. Be thankful unto him, and bless his name.

For the Lord is gracious, his mercy is everlasting, and his truth endureth from generation to generation.

O God! we adore thee as our God, as our Creator, and as the Father of our Lord Jesus Christ.

We humble ourselves in thy presence, and acknowledge thine infinite majesty.

The angels adore thee in heaven, and all the heavenly host bow down before thee.

Receive the homage which we offer to thee upon earth, we who are poor mortals, miserable sinners, thy creatures by nature, and thy children by grace.

Glory be to the Father, and to the Son, and to the Holy Ghost; as it was in the beginning, is now, and ever shall be, world without end. *Amen.*

Seventh Canticle.

COME and let us present ourselves before the Lord; let us adore him in his temple; let us humble ourselves in his sanctuary.

The Lord is here. How venerable, how sacred is this place! this is the house of God; this is the gate of heaven.

O Lord! God of our fathers, thou art blessed for ever. To thee belong greatness, power, glory, eternity, majesty.

All that is in heaven and in earth is thine: the kingdom is thine.

Thou art a Prince above all things: thou art Sovereign over all. Riches and honour, power and might, are in thy hand.

Now therefore, O our God! we magnify thee, and praise thy glorious name.

Who are we, and who are this people, that we are enabled freely to offer unto thee this service, and this praise?

We are strangers before thee, and our days pass away as a shadow.

Although we are but dust and ashes, behold, we take upon ourselves to speak unto thee.

Let the words of our mouths be acceptable unto thee, O Lord!

Let thy mercy be upon us, O God! as our trust is in thee.

Glory be, &c.

Eighth Canticle.

HOW amiable are thy tabernacles, O Lord of Hosts. My soul desireth, yea, even longeth, to enter into the courts of the Lord. My heart and my flesh rejoice in the living God.

Blessed are they that dwell in thy house: they will be always praising thee.

One day in thy courts is better than a thousand elsewhere: I would rather be a door-keeper in the house of my God, than to dwell in the tents of ungodliness.

For the Lord God is a sun and a shield: no good thing will he withhold from them that walk uprightly.

O Lord of Hosts! blessed is the man that trusteth in thee.

O God! I will abide in thy tabernacle for ever: I will trust in the covert of thy wings.

For thou, O God! hast heard my vows; thou hast given me the heritage of those who fear thy name.

I am ever with thee: thou hast holden me by thy right hand.

Thou wilt guide me with thy counsel, and afterward receive me to glory.

Whom have I in heaven but thee? and there is none upon earth that I desire besides thee.

They that forsake thee shall perish: thou wilt destroy all them that corrupt themselves before thee.

But it is good for me to draw near unto God; and to put my trust in the Lord God.

Glory be, &c.

Ninth Canticle.

O GOD! thou art my God, early do I seek thee: my soul thirsteth for thee, my flesh longeth after thee in a dry and barren land.

I desire to see thy power and thy glory, in thy sanctuary.

Blessed is the man whom thou choosest, and causest to approach unto thee, that he may dwell in thy courts.

Blessed be God, the Father of our Lord Jesus Christ, who, according to his abundant mercy, hath begotten us again unto a lively hope, by the resurrection of Jesus Christ from the dead;

To an inheritance incorruptible, undefiled, and that fadeth not away, reserved in heaven for us.

Blessed be the Lord God, the God of Israel, who only doeth wondrous things.

And blessed be his glorious name for ever: and let the whole earth be filled with his glory.

Blessed be the Lord, from one generation to another: and let all the people say, Amen.

Glory be, &c.

Tenth Canticle.

O YE servants of the Lord, praise the name of the Lord.

Blessed be the name of the Lord, from this time forth and for ever more.

From the rising of the sun, even unto the going down of the same, the Lord's name is to be praised.

The Lord is high above all nations, and his glory above the heavens.

Who is like unto the Lord our God, who dwelleth on high; and yet humbleth himself to behold the things that are in heaven and earth.

The Lord is merciful and gracious, slow to anger, and of great goodness.

He hath not dealt with us after our sins, nor rewarded us according to our iniquities.

God, who is rich in mercy, for his great love wherewith he loved us, even when we were dead in sins, hath quickened us together with Christ;

Unto him be glory in the Church, by Christ Jesus, throughout all ages, world without end.

Glory be, &c.

Eleventh Canticle.

I WILL sing of the mercies of the Lord. With my mouth will I make known thy faithfulness to all generations.

O Lord God of Hosts! who is like unto thee? Thou hast a mighty arm; strong is thy hand, and high is thy right hand.

Justice and judgment are the foundation of thy throne: mercy and truth go before thy face.

Great and marvellous are thy works, Lord God Almighty! Just and true are thy ways, thou king of saints!

Who would not fear thee, O Lord! and glorify thy name? For thou only art holy.

All nations shall come and worship before thee; for thy judgments are made manifest.

Rejoice in the Lord, ye righteous, and give thanks at the remembrance of his holiness.

Praise his name, which is great, and greatly to be feared, for it is holy.

Praise the power of the King, who loveth righteousness.

Exalt the Lord our God; and worship at his footstool, for he is holy.

Praise him in psalms, and hymns, and spiritual songs, singing and making melody in your heart unto the Lord.

Give thanks always for all things, unto our God and Father, in the name of our Lord Jesus Christ.

Glory be, &c.

Twelfth Canticle.

I WILL bless the Lord at all times: his praise shall continually be in my mouth.

My soul shall glory in the Lord; the humble shall hear thereof and be glad.

O! magnify the Lord with me, and let us exalt his name together.

O taste and see how gracious the Lord is! Blessed is the man that trusteth in him.

Thy mercy, O Lord! reacheth unto the heavens, and thy truth unto the clouds.

Thy righteousness is like the great mountains; thy judgments are like the great deep! O Lord! thou preservest man and beast.

How excellent is thy loving-kindness, O God!

Therefore, the children of men put their trust under the shadow of thy wings.

They shall be satisfied with the plenteousness of thy house; and thou shalt make them drink of the river of thy pleasure.

For with thee is the fountain of life: and in thy light shall we see light.

O continue thy loving-kindness unto them that know thee; and thy righteousness unto the upright in heart.

Now unto him, that is able to keep us from falling, and to present us faultless, before the presence of his glory, with exceeding joy:

To the only wise God, our Saviour, be glory and majesty, dominion and power, both now and for ever.

Glory be to the Father, and to the Son, and to the Holy Ghost; as it was in the beginning, is now, and ever shall be, world without end. *Amen.*

Thirteenth Canticle.

O LORD! let our prayer be set forth in thy sight, as incense; and the lifting up of our hands, be as the evening sacrifice.

Bless ye the Lord, all ye servants of the Lord; ye who worship in the house of the Lord.

Lift up your hands in the sanctuary, and bless the Lord.

Praise ye the Lord, sing praises unto our God; for it is a pleasant thing to be thankful.

Our Lord is above all: whatever he pleaseth, that doeth he, in heaven and in earth, in the sea, and in all deep places.

Bless the Lord, O house of Israel! Bless the Lord, O house of Aaron! Bless the Lord, O house of Levi! Ye that fear the Lord, bless the Lord.

God having raised up his Son Jesus, sent him to bless us, in turning away every one of us from his iniquities.

Thanks be unto God, for his unspeakable gift.

We give thanks to thee, O God! who art the Father of our Lord Jesus Christ, for the hope which is laid up for us in heaven.

Glory be to the Father, and to the Son, and to the Holy Ghost; as it was in the beginning, is now, and ever shall be, world without end. *Amen.*

Fourteenth Canticle.

IT is a good thing to give thanks unto the Lord, and to sing praises unto thy name, O Most High!

To show forth thy loving-kindness in the morning, and thy faithfulness every night.

O Lord! thou hast made us glad through thy works, and we will rejoice in the operations of thy hands.

O Lord! how glorious are thy works! Thy thoughts are very deep.

O Lord our God! thou art clothed with majesty and honour.

Manifold are thy works; in wisdom hast thou made them all.

The earth is full of thy riches.

The heavens declare thy glory, and the firmament showeth thy handy work.

The glory of the Lord will endure for ever:—the Lord will rejoice in his works.

Let all those who fear him bless him, saying, Holy, Holy, Holy, Lord God Almighty! who wast, and art, and art to come.

Thou art worthy to receive glory, and honour, and power; for thou hast created all things, and for thy pleasure they were created.

Wherefore we bless thee, O Eternal God! Creator and Redeemer of the world, we magnify thy power and extol thy mercy.

Glory be, &c.

Fifteenth Canticle.

COME ye and bless the Lord your God, for ever and ever: and blessed, O God! be thy glorious name.

Thou, Lord, in the beginning, didst lay the foundation of the earth, and the heavens are the work of thy hands:

They shall perish, but thou remainest; they all shall wax old, and shall be changed; but thou art forever the same, and thy years shall not fail.

All thy works shall praise thee, O Lord! thy saints shall bless thee.

The works of the Lord are great; sought out of all them that have pleasure therein.

His works are full of majesty and glory; his righteousness endureth for ever.

The Lord is full of compassion; his tender mercies are over all his works.

He hath remembered his covenant; he hath sent redemption unto his people; holy and reverend is his name.

Let all creatures praise the Lord, and let him be for ever blessed in the congregation of the saints.

Glory be to the Father, and to the Son, and to the Holy Ghost; as it was in the beginning, is now, and ever shall be, world without end. *Amen.*

Sixteenth Canticle.

O! COME, let us worship the Lord; let us praise him, and give him thanks for all his benefits.

O Lord, our God! how excellent is thy name, in all the earth. Thy glory is above the heavens.

Lord! what is man, that thou art mindful of him, and the son of man, that thou visitest him?

Lord Jesus! thou art the only Son of the Father: thou art God over all, blessed forever.

Thou art the image of the invisible God: the first born of all creatures.

By thee were all things created, that are in heaven and earth: Thou wast before all things, and by thee do all things subsist.

Thou art seated at the right hand of the Father. Thou hast all power in heaven and earth:

And we know that thou shalt come in thy glory, to judge the quick and the dead.

We place our trust in thee, O our Saviour! and offer unto thee our thanks.

Unto him that loved us, and gave himself for us, be glory and dominion for ever and ever.

Glory be to the Father, and to the Son, and to the Holy Ghost; as it was in the beginning, is now, and ever shall be, world without end. *Amen.*

Seventeenth Canticle.

SING unto the Lord, bless his name: show forth his salvation from day to day.

For the Lord is great, and greatly to be praised: he is to be feared above all gods.

The gods of the nations are idols; but the Lord made the heavens.

Majesty and glory are before him : power and excellence are in his sanctuary.

Ascribe unto the Lord, O ye people! ascribe unto the Lord, glory and honour.

Ascribe unto the Lord, the honour due unto his name: bring your offerings and come into his courts.

O! worship the Lord in the beauty of holiness; let the whole earth stand in awe of him.

Declare through all the earth, the Lord reigneth; with righteousness will he judge the world, and the people with equity.

Blessed be the Lord God of Israel, for he hath visited and redeemed his people.

Blessed be the God and Father of our Lord Jesus Christ, who hath blessed us with all spiritual blessings, in heavenly places, in Christ.

Glory be to the Father, and to the Son, and to the Holy Ghost; as it was in the beginning, is now and ever shall be, world without end. *Amen.*

Eighteenth Canticle.

THE TE DEUM.

WE praise thee, O God! we acknowledge thee to be the Lord.

All the earth doth worship thee, the Father everlasting.

To thee all Angels cry aloud; the Heavens, and all the Powers therein.

To thee, Cherubim and Seraphim continually do cry,

Holy, holy, holy, Lord God of Sabaoth.

Heaven and earth are full of the majesty of thy glory.

The glorious company of the Apostles praise thee.

The goodly fellowship of the Prophets praise thee.

The noble army of Martyrs praise thee.

The holy Church, throughout all the world, doth acknowledge thee,

The Father, of an infinite Majesty;

Thine adorable, true, and only Son;

Also the Holy Ghost, the Comforter.

Thou art the King of Glory, O Christ!

Thou art the everlasting Son of the Father.

When thou tookest upon thee to deliver man, thou didst humble thyself to be born of a Virgin.

When thou hadst overcome the sharpness of death, thou didst open the kingdom of heaven to all believers.

Thou sittest at the right hand of God, in the glory of the Father.

We believe that thou shalt come to be our Judge.

We therefore pray thee, help thy servants, whom thou hast redeemed with thy precious blood.

Make them to be numbered with thy saints, in glory everlasting.

O Lord! save thy people, and bless thine heritage.

Govern them, and lift them up for ever.

Day by day we magnify thee;

And we worship thy name ever, world without end.

Vouchsafe, O Lord, to keep us this day without sin.

O Lord! have mercy upon us, have mercy upon us.

O Lord! let thy mercy be upon us, as our trust is in thee.

O Lord! in thee have I trusted; let me never be confounded.

Nineteenth Canticle.

Psalm LXVII.

GOD be merciful unto us, and bless us, and show us the light of his countenance, and be merciful unto us;

That thy way may be known upon earth, thy saving health among all nations.

Let the people praise thee, O God! yea, let all the people praise thee.

O let the nations rejoice and be glad; for thou shalt judge the folk righteously, and govern the nations upon earth.

Let the people praise thee, O God! yea, let all the people praise thee.

Then shall the earth bring forth her increase; and God, even our own God, shall give us his blessing.

God shall bless us, and all the ends of the world shall fear him.

Twentieth Canticle.

Psalm C.

O BE joyful in the Lord, all ye lands: serve the Lord with gladness, and come before his presence with a song.

Be ye sure that the Lord he is God: it is he that hath made us, and not we ourselves; we are his people, and the sheep of his pasturė.

O go your way into his gates with thanksgiving, and into his courts with praise; be thankful unto him, and speak good of his name.

For the Lord is gracious, his mercy is everlasting; and his truth endureth from generation to generation.

Twenty-First Canticle.

From Psalm CIII.

PRAISE the Lord, O my soul, and all that is within me, praise his holy name.

Praise the Lord, O my soul, and forget not all his benefits:

Who forgiveth all thy sin, and healeth all thine infirmities;

Who saveth thy life from destruction, and crowneth thee with mercy and loving-kindness.

O praise the Lord, ye angels of his, ye that excel in strength; ye that fulfil his commandment, and hearken unto the voice of his word.

O praise the Lord, all ye his hosts; ye servants of his that do his pleasure.

O speak good of the Lord, all ye works of his, in all places of his dominion: praise thou the Lord, O my soul.

Twenty-Second Canticle.

Psalm CL.

O PRAISE God in his holiness: praise him in the firmament of his power.

Praise him in his noble acts: praise him according to his excellent greatness.

Praise him in the sound of the trumpet: praise him upon the lute and harp.

Praise him in the cymbals and dances: praise him upon the strings and pipe.

Praise him upon the well-tuned cymbals: praise him upon the loud cymbals.

Let every thing that hath breath praise the Lord.

Canticles for Holy Days and for Particular Occasions.

Twenty-Third Canticle.

FOR THE EVE OF THE NATIVITY.

SING unto the Lord a new song: let his praise be declared throughout the earth and in the sea.

Let the wilderness and the cities lift up their voice: let them rejoice with songs of triumph.

Let them give glory unto the Lord: let them make known his praises among the isles.

The Lord hath comforted his people: and all the ends of the earth shall see the salvation of our God.

Say ye to the Daughter of Zion: behold, thy Saviour cometh: behold, his reward is with him.

Unto you, that fear my name, shall the Sun of Righteousness arise, with healing in his wings.

The glory of the Lord shall be revealed: and all flesh shall see it together.

Death shail be swallowed up in victory: and the Lord God will wipe away all tears from our eyes.

In that day shall it be said : Lo ! this is our God : we have waited for him, and he will save us.

Lo ! this is the Lord : we will rejoice in his salvation.

Blessed is he that cometh in the name of the Lord.

Glory be, &c.

Twenty-Fourth Canticle.

FOR THE DAY OF THE NATIVITY.

BEHOLD ! I bring you good tidings of great joy.

For unto you is born this day, in the city of David, a Saviour, which is Christ, the Lord !

Glory to God in the highest, on earth peace, good will towards men.

Unto us a Child is born, unto us a Son is given; and the government shall be on his shoulders;

And his name shall be called Wonderful, Counsellor, the Mighty God, the Everlasting Father, the Prince of Peace.

God hath remembered his covenant : he hath sent redemption unto his people.

Israel hath been saved in the Lord, with an everlasting salvation.

This is the Lord's doing, and it is marvellous in our eyes.

This is the day, which the Lord hath made : we will rejoice and be glad in it.

Behold, now is the accepted time; behold, now is the day of salvation.

Let it be said throughout the earth, the Lord reigneth; let the heavens rejoice, let the earth be glad.

For with righteousness will he judge the world, and the people with his truth.

Blessed be he, that cometh in the name of the Lord; Hosannah in the highest.

Glory be, &c.

Twenty-Fifth Canticle.

FOR THE DAY OF THE NATIVITY.

BLESSED be the Lord God of Israel, for he hath visited and redeemed his people;

And hath raised up a horn of salvation for us, in the house of his servant David.

As he spake by the mouth of his holy prophets, that we should be saved from our enemies, and from the hand of all that hate us;

To perform the mercy promised to our fathers, and to remember his holy covenant:

The oath which he sware unto our father Abraham,

That he would grant unto us, that we, being delivered out of the hand of our enemies, might serve him, without fear,

In holiness and righteousness, all the days of our life.

He hath given knowledge of salvation unto his people, by the remission of their sins,

Through the tender mercy of our God, whereby the day spring from on high hath visited us,

To give light to them that sit in darkness, and in the shadow of death; to guide our feet into the way of peace.

Glory be, &c.

Twenty-Sixth Canticle

FOR THE DAY AFTER THE NATIVITY.

SING unto the Lord a new song, for he hath done marvellous things.

His right hand, and his holy arm hath gotten him the victory.

The Lord hath made known his salvation: his righteousness hath he openly showed in the sight of the heathen.

He hath remembered his mercy and his truth.

Show yourselves joyful unto the Lord, all ye lands; rejoice and sing praises.

Let the sea make a noise, and all that therein is, the world and they that dwell therein.

Let the floods clap their hands, and let the hills be joyful together before the Lord, for he cometh to judge the earth.

With righteousness shall he judge the world, and the people with equity.

This is a faithful saying, and worthy of all acceptation, that Jesus Christ came into the world to save sinners.

Lord! now lettest thou thy servants depart in peace.

For our eyes have seen thy salvation, which thou hast prepared before the face of all people:

A light to lighten the Gentiles, and the glory of thy people Israel.

Glory be, &c.

Twenty-Seventh Canticle.

FOR THE DAY OF THE CRUCIFIXION.

CHRIST our Passover was sacrificed for us. He was delivered for our offences.

He bare our sins in his body on the tree: and God hath laid on him the iniquity of us all.

His soul was exceedingly sorrowful, even unto death:

He was brought as a lamb to the slaughter: he humbled himself even unto the death of the cross.

He was taken away through the force of agony and of condemnation; and he was cut off out of the land of the living.

Worthy is the Lamb that was slain, to receive

power, and riches, and wisdom, and strength, and honour, and glory, and blessing for ever and ever.

Let every creature that is in heaven, and on the earth, give praise and honour to him, that sitteth on the throne, and unto the Lamb.

Now is come the kingdom of God, and the power of his Christ.

Glory be, &c.

Twenty-Eighth Canticle.

FOR THE DAY OF THE CRUCIFIXION.

LET us bless God, our Father, for the gift of his Son, through whom we have redemption, even the remission of our sins.

Lord Jesus! thou gavest thyself for us, that thou mightest deliver us from this present evil world, according to the will of God, our Father.

Knowing that in burnt offerings and sacrifices, God had no pleasure;

Thou saidst, Lo! I come; in the volume of the book it is written of me, to do thy will, O God!

After thou hadst offered one sacrifice for sin, thou didst sit down for ever, at the right hand of God.

For by this one offering thou hast perfected for ever them that are sanctified.

Thy throne, O God! endureth for ever and ever; a sceptre of righteousness is the sceptre of thy kingdom.

Thou hast loved righteousness; therefore God, even thy God, hath anointed thee with the oil of gladness above thy fellows.

Who shall lay any thing to the charge of God's elect! It is God that justifieth.

Who is he that condemneth? It is Christ that died; yea rather that is risen again.

He died for our offences, and was raised again for our justification.

Glory be, &c.

Twenty-Ninth Canticle.

FOR THE DAY OF THE RESURRECTION.

CHRIST our Passover was sacrificed for us:

Therefore, let us keep the feast, not with the leaven of wickedness and hypocrisy, but with the unleavened bread of sincerity and truth.

Christ, being raised from the dead, dieth no more; death hath no more dominion over him.

He died unto sin once, but now he liveth unto God.

Being the Prince of life, it was not possible that he should be holden of the bonds of death.

God hath not left his soul in the place of departed spirits; neither hath he suffered his Holy One to see corruption.

He was dead, but he liveth for ever more; and hath the keys of hell and of death.

Christ is risen from the dead, and become the first fruits of them that sleep.

Since by man came death, by man came also the resurrection of the dead: and as in Adam all die, even so in Christ shall all be made alive.

Death is swallowed up in victory. O death! where is thy sting? O grave! where is thy victory?

Thanks be to God, who giveth us the victory, through our Lord Jesus Christ.

Glory be, &c.

Thirtieth Canticle.

FOR THE DAY OF THE RESURRECTION.

THIS is a faithful saying, and worthy of all acceptation, that Jesus Christ came into the world to save sinners.

Therefore, we will sing hymns in honour of our God; and praise him above all, for ever and ever.

Who spared not his own Son.

Who ordained that he should be despised and rejected of men, a man of sorrows and acquainted with grief;

That he should be wounded for our transgressions, and bruised for our iniquities;

That the chastisement of our peace should be upon him; and that by his stripes we should be healed.

Forasmuch as children are partakers of flesh and

blood, he became partaker of the same; that, through his death, he might destroy him that had the power of death;

And deliver them, who through fear of death, were all their life time subject to bondage.

Now is come salvation and strength, the kingdom of our God and the power of his Christ.

We see Jesus, who was made a little lower than the angels, crowned with glory and honour; that he, by the grace of God, should taste death for every man.

Let us sing the new song of those who were redeemed from among men, being the first fruits unto God and to the Lamb.

Let us fear God, and give glory to him: let us worship him who made heaven and earth, and the sea, and the fountains of waters.

Glory be, &c.

Thirty-First Canticle.

FOR THE DAY OF THE RESURRECTION.

O TASTE and see that the Lord is gracious.

Coming unto him, as unto a living stone; disallowed indeed of men, but chosen of God, and precious;

Ye also as living stones are built up a spiritual house, a holy priesthood, to offer up spiritual sacrifices, acceptable to God, through Jesus Christ.

Ye, who in time past were not his people, but are now the people of God; ye, who had not obtained mercy, but now have obtained mercy;

Consider well, that ye were not redeemed with corruptible things, as silver and gold, from your vain conversation;

But with the precious blood of Christ, as of a lamb without blemish and without spot.

By him ye believe in God, that raised him up from the dead, and gave him glory, that your faith and hope might be in God.

Let us bless him that cometh in the name of the Lord.

Though he were the Son of God, yet learned he obedience, by the things which he suffered:

And being made perfect, he became the author of eternal salvation, unto all them that obey him.

Having therefore, brethren, liberty to enter into the holiest, by the blood of Jesus;

Let us draw near with a true heart, in full assurance of faith, having our hearts sprinkled from an evil conscience.

Through him, we have access, by one Spirit, unto the Father.

Now unto him that is able to do exceeding abundantly, above all that we ask or think, according to the power that worketh in us; unto him be glory in the Church, throughout all ages.

Glory be, &c.

Thirty-Second Canticle.

FOR THE DAY OF THE RESURRECTION.

LET us worship him who liveth for ever and ever. Let all creatures which are in heaven, and on the earth, and under the earth, and such as are in the sea, and all that are in them, say,

Blessing and honour, and glory and power, be unto him that sitteth on the throne, and to the Lamb, for ever and ever.

God so loved the world, that he gave his only begotten Son, that whosoever believeth in him should not perish, but have everlasting life.

God commendeth his love towards us, in that while we were yet sinners, Christ died for us.

If when we were enemies, we were reconciled to God by the death of his Son, much more being reconciled, shall we be saved by his life.

Christ also hath once suffered for sins, the just for the unjust, that he might bring us to God; being put to death in the flesh, but quickened by the Spirit.

He bare our sins in his own body, on the tree, that we being dead to sin, should live unto righteousness; by whose stripes we are healed.

Wherefore we bless thee, O Lord God, Creator and Redeemer of the world, we extol thy power and praise thy mercy.

Blessed be the God and Father of our Lord

Jesus Christ, who, according to his abundant mercy, hath begotten us again unto a lively hope, by the resurrection of Jesus Christ from the dead.

Glory be, &c.

Thirty-Third Canticle.

FOR THE DAY OF THE ASCENSION.

THE Lord said unto my Lord, sit thou at my right hand, until I make thine enemies thy footstool.

The Lord shall send the rod of thy strength out of Zion, saying, rule thou in the midst of thine enemies.

The Lord hath sworn and will not repent, thou art a priest for ever, after the order of Melchizedek.

O! clap your hands, all ye people: shout unto God with the voice of triumph.

God is gone up with rejoicing, the Lord hath gone up with the song of victory.

Lift up your heads, O ye gates, and be ye lift up, ye everlasting doors, and the King of Glory shall come in.

Who is the King of Glory? It is the Lord, strong and mighty; he is the King of Glory.

Sing praises unto God, sing praises unto our King; for God is the King of all the earth; he reigneth over the nations; he sitteth upon the throne of his holiness.

Let all men bow down before him, and let all the angels of God worship him.

Thy throne, O God! is for ever and ever: a sceptre of righteousness is the sceptre of thy kingdom.

Thou didst ascend up on high; thou didst lead captivity captive; thou hast received gifts for men.

Thou art gone to thy Father's house, to prepare mansions for us.

Glory be, &c.

Thirty-Fourth Canticle.

FOR THE EVE OF THE ASCENSION, AND THE DAY AFTER.

THE Lord reigneth; let the people tremble; he sitteth between the cherubim; let the earth be moved.

He is high above all the earth; he is exalted far above all the heavens.

God, the Father of our Lord Jesus Christ, hath highly exalted him, and given him a name, which is above every name:

That, at the name of Jesus, every knee should bow, of things in heaven, and things on earth, and things under the earth:

And that every tongue should confess, that Jesus Christ is Lord, to the glory of God, the Father.

All power hath been given unto him in heaven and on earth. God hath put all things under his feet, and gave him to be the head over all things to the Church.

We have liberty to enter into the holiest, by the blood of Jesus, by a new and living way, which he hath consecrated for us, through the vail, that is to say, his flesh.

Let us draw near with a true heart, in full assurance of faith, having our hearts purified from an evil conscience, and our bodies washed with pure water.

Let us come with confidence unto the throne of grace, that we may obtain mercy and help in time of need.

Glory be to the Father, and to the Son, and to the Holy Ghost; as it was in the beginning, is now, and ever shall be, world without end. *Amen.*

Thirty-Fifth Canticle.

FOR PENTECOST.

NOT unto us, O Lord! not unto us, but unto thy name, give glory.

Our God is in heaven: he doth whatsoever pleaseth him.

The Lord hath been mindful of us: he will bless them that fear him, both small and great.

Ye are blessed of the Lord, who made heaven and earth.

He hath poured out his Spirit upon the posterity of his people.

He hath put in them a new spirit, that they should walk in his commandments, and keep his laws;

To the end, that they might be his people, and that he might be their God.

Who is so great a God as our God? Thou art the God that doest wonders.

Thou hast poured out thy Spirit upon all flesh.

For to one, thou hast given by the Spirit, the word of wisdom; to another, the word of knowledge by the same Spirit;

To another, faith by the same Spirit; to another, prophecy.

All these worketh that one and the self same Spirit, dividing to every man separately, as it hath pleased him.

Blessed be the God and Father of our Lord Jesus Christ, who hath blessed us with all spiritual blessings, in heavenly places, in Christ:

According as he hath chosen us in him, before the foundation of the world, that we should be holy and without blame before him.

Glory be, &c.

Thirty-Sixth Canticle.

FOR PENTECOST.

BLESSED be the Lord our God, for he hath shown marvellous kindness.

The Lord hath remembered his mercy and truth.

Having exalted his Son to his right hand, he hath fulfilled this promise:

I will pour out my Spirit upon all flesh: your sons and your daughters shall prophecy.

On my servants and on my hand maidens, I will pour out my Spirit.

This promise was unto our fathers and to their children, and to all that were afar off, even as many as the Lord, our God, shall call.

Wherefore, O our God! we bless thee as our benefactor, and thou shalt ever be the subject of our songs.

We will speak of thy greatness; we will make known every where the remembrance of thy loving-kindness.

Thy mercy, O Lord! reacheth unto the heavens, and thy faithfulness unto the clouds!

Ho! all ye that thirst, come unto the waters.

Blessed are they that do hunger and thirst after righteousness; for they shall be filled.

Our Father, who is in heaven, giveth his Holy Spirit to them that ask him.

O God! turn thy face from our sins, and blot out our iniquities.

O God! create in us clean hearts, and renew a right spirit within us.

Cast us not away from thy presence, and take not thy Holy Spirit from us.

Let thy loving Spirit lead us forth into the land of righteousness.

Glory be, &c.

Thirty-Seventh Canticle.

FOR PENTECOST.

THERE is therefore now no condemnation to them that are in Christ Jesus; who walk not after the flesh but after the Spirit.

The law of the Spirit of life, in Christ Jesus, hath made them free from the law of sin and death.

We have received, not the spirit of the world, but the Spirit which is of God; that we might know the things that are freely given to us of God.

The natural man receiveth not the Spirit of God, for they are foolishness unto him; neither can he know them, because they are spiritually discerned.

But he that is spiritual judgeth all things.

Let us aim at spiritual gifts. For they that are after the flesh do mind the things of the flesh; but they that are after the Spirit, the things of the Spirit.

But we are not in the flesh, but in the Spirit, if so be, that the Spirit of God dwelleth in us.

This Spirit, which God sendeth into our hearts, convinceth us that we are no longer in bondage, but that we are his children, and if children, then heirs of God, through Jesus Christ.

If the Spirit of him that raised up Jesus from the dead, dwell in us, he that raised up Christ from the dead, shall also quicken our mortal bodies, by his Spirit that dwelleth in us.

Glory be, &c.

Thirty-Eighth Canticle.

FOR THE HOLY DAYS OF SEPTEMBER.

O GIVE thanks unto the Lord, for he is good; his mercy endureth for ever.

Let them that fear the Lord, now say that his mercy endureth for ever.

The Lord is our strength, and the subject of our songs; he is our Redeemer.

The Lord hath done marvellous things.

He hath remembered his covenant; he hath visited and redeemed his people.

God so loved the world, that he gave his only begotten Son; that whosoever believeth in him should not perish, but have everlasting life.

Let us praise him, let us glorify and bless his name.

Let us give thanks unto God our Father, who hath made us meet to be partakers of the inheritance of the saints in light.

Salvation cometh from our God, that sitteth upon the throne, and from the Lamb, for ever and ever. Amen.

Blessing, glory, wisdom, thanksgiving, honour, power and strength, be unto our God, for ever and ever.

Praise our God, all ye his servants, both small and great.

The Lord our God Omnipotent reigneth; and we shall reign with him, for ever and ever.

Glory be to the Father, and to the Son, and to the Holy Ghost; as it was in the beginning, is now, and ever shall be, world without end. *Amen.*

Thirty-Ninth Canticle.

FOR THE HOLY DAYS OF SEPTEMBER.

IN this was manifested the love of God towards us; because that God sent his only begotten Son into the world, that we might live through him.

Herein is love, not that we loved God, but that he loved us, and sent his Son to be the propitiation for our sins.

Let us love God, because he first loved us.

The Lord hath remembered his mercy and truth, for they endure for ever.

For thy name's sake, O Lord! be merciful unto our sins, although they are great.

Behold what manner of love the Father hath bestowed upon us, that we should be called the children of God;

And if children, then heirs; heirs of God, and joint heirs with Christ.

Since we call upon him as a Father, who, without respect of persons, judgeth according to every man's work; let us pass the time of our sojourning here in fear.

Let the name of our Lord Jesus Christ be glorified in us, and let us be glorified in him, according to the grace of our God, and the Lord Jesus Christ.

Glory be, &c.

Fortieth Canticle.

FOR THE COMMUNION.

WE will praise thee, O God! we will exalt thy name for ever;

For all the earth is full of thy goodness, of thy glory and of thy mercy.

Bless the Lord, O my soul, and all that is within me, praise his holy name.

Who forgiveth all thy sin, and healeth all thine infirmities.

The Lord is full of compassion and mercy, long suffering and of great goodness.

He hath not dealt with us after our sins, nor rewarded us according to our iniquities.

For as the heaven is high above the earth, so great is his mercy towards them that fear him.

As far as the east is from the west, so far hath he removed our transgressions from us.

Yea, like as a Father pitieth his own children, even so, is the Lord merciful unto us.

For when we were his enemies, and while we were yet sinners, he gave us his only begotten Son, that we might live through him.

He that spared not his own Son, but delivered him up to die for us all, how shall he not with him also, freely give us all things.

Let my heart and my mouth show forth the praises of the Lord.

Glory be, &c.

Forty-First Canticle.

FOR THE COMMUNION.

LET us praise the Lord our God, and extol his mercy towards his people, and towards his elect.

He showeth his word unto Jacob, his statutes and judgments unto Israel:

He hath not dealt so with any nation.

Thou also, O God! art praised in Zion, and unto thee is the vow of thy people performed.

Blessed are the people, O Lord! who rejoice in thee; they shall walk in the light of thy countenance.

Their delight shall be daily in thy name; and in thy righteousness shall they make their boast.

We, who in times past, were not his people, are now the people of God.

He hath made us a chosen generation, a royal priesthood, a holy nation, a peculiar people;

That we should show forth the praises of him who hath called us out of darkness, unto his marvellous light.

Herein will our Father be glorified, if we bear

much fruit: so shall we be truly the disciples of his Son.

We shall abide in his love, until he shall come to be glorified in his saints, and to be admired in all them that believe.

Glory be, etc.

Forty-Second Canticle.

FOR THE COMMUNION.

O! COME and hear, all ye that fear God, and I will declare what he hath done for my soul.

The Lord hath remembered his tender mercies and his loving-kindnesses, which have been ever of old.

Our misdeeds had prevailed against us: thou hast taken away our transgressions.

God is not willing that any should perish, but that all should come to repentance.

He sent his Son to give repentance to Israel, and forgiveness of sins.

In this was manifested the love of God towards us, because that God sent his only begotten Son into the world, that we might live through him.

Let us show forth the Lord's death, till he come.

The bread, which we break, is it not the communion of the body of Christ?

The cup of blessing, which we bless, is it not the communion of the blood of Christ?

To me, to live is Christ, and to die is gain.
Thanks be unto God, for this unspeakable gift.
Glory be, &c.

Forty-Third Canticle.

FOR THE COMMUNION.

O! GIVE thanks unto the Lord, for he is good, for his mercy endureth for ever.

Let the redeemed of the Lord say so; such as sat in darkness, and in the shadow of death;

Who had rebelled against the word of God, and contemned the counsel of the Most High.

He hath brought them out of darkness, and the shadow of death; he hath broken their bonds in-sunder.

O that men would therefore praise the Lord for his goodness, and for his wonderful works to the children of men!

This salvation hath been declared in the Gospel of Jesus Christ,

Who, of God, is made unto us wisdom, and righteousness, and sanctification, and redemption.

How beautiful upon the mountains are the feet of him that bringeth good tidings, that publisheth peace;

That bringeth good tidings of good, that publisheth salvation; that saith unto Zion, thy God reigneth.

Let us thank God always for the grace which is given us through Jesus Christ;

That in every thing being enriched by him, we may be wanting in no gift, waiting for the coming of our Lord Jesus Christ.

God is faithful, by whom we are called unto the fellowship of his Son Jesus Christ.

Blessed is the people whom the Lord hath chosen for his own inheritance.

He that glorieth, let him glory in the Lord.

Glory be to the Father, and to the Son, and to the Holy Ghost; as it was in the beginning, is now, and ever shall be, world without end. *Amen.*

CONFESSION DE FOI,

FAIT D'UN COMMUN ACCORD PAR LES

EGLISES REFORMEES DU ROYAUME DE FRANCE.

ARTICLE I.

Nous croyons et confessons qu'il y a un seul Dieu, qui est une seule et simple essence, spirituelle, éternelle, invisible, immuable, infinie, incompréhensible, ineffable, qui peut toutes choses, qui est toute sage, toute bonne, toute juste, et toute miséricordieuse.

II.—Ce Dieu se manifeste tel aux hommes, premierement, par ses œuvres, tant par la création que par la conservation et conduite d'icelles. Secondement et plus clairement par sa Parole, laquelle au commencement revelée par Oracles, a été puis aprés redigée par écrit aux livres que nous appellons l'Ecriture Sainte.

III.—Toute cette Ecriture Sainte est comprise aux livres Canoniques du Vieux et Nouveau Testament: desquels le nombre s'ensuit. Les cinq Livres de Moïse ; assavoir Genese, Exode, Levitique, Nombres, Deuteronome. Item, Josué,

CONFESSION OF FAITH,

MADE BY COMMON CONSENT OF THE

REFORMED CHURCHES OF THE KINGDOM OF FRANCE.

ARTICLE I.

We believe and confess that there is but one God, who is a single and simple essence, spiritual, eternal, invisible, immutable, infinite, incomprehensible, ineffable, omnipotent, who is all-wise, all-good, all-just, and all-merciful.

II.—This God manifests himself such unto men: first, by his works, as well in their creation, as in their preservation and government. Secondly, and more clearly, by his word, which, revealed in the beginning by oracles, was afterwards reduced to writing, in the books which we call the Holy Scriptures.

III.—These Holy Scriptures are comprised in the Canonical Books of the Old and New Testament, the number of which is as follows: The five Books of Moses: namely, Genesis, Exodus, Leviticus, Numbers, Deuteronomy; also Joshua,

Juges, Ruth, le premier et second livre de Samuel, le premier et second livre des Rois, le premier et second livre des Croniques, autrement dits Paralipomenon, le premier livre d'Esdras. Item, Nehemie, de livre d'Esther, Job, les Pseaumes de David, les Proverbes où Sentences de Salomon: le livre de l'Ecclesiaste, dit le Précheur, le Cantique de Salomon. Item, le livre d'Esaïe, Jeremie, Lamentations de Jeremie, Ezechiel, Daniel, Osée, Joël, Amos, Abdias, Jonas, Michée, Nahum, Abakuc, Sophonie, Aggée, Zacharie, Malachie. Item, le Saint Evangile, selon S. Matthieu, selon S. Marc, selon S. Luc, et selon S. Jean. Item, le second livre de S. Luc, autrement dit les Actes des Apôtres. Item, les Epitres de S. Paul, aux Romains une, aux Corinthiens deux, aux Galates une, aux Ephésiens une, aux Philippiens une, aux Colossiens une, aux Thessaloniciens deux, à Timothée deux, à Tite une, à Philemon une. Item, l'Epitre aux Hebreux, l'Epitre de S. Jaques, la premiere et seconde Epitre de S. Pierre, la premiere deuxième et troisième Epitre de S. Jean, l'Epitre de S. Jude. Item, l'Apocalypse ou Revelation de S. Jean.

Judges, Ruth, the first and second book of Samuel, the first and second book of Kings, the first and second book of Chronicles, otherwise called Paralipomenon. The first book of Esdras, also, Nehemiah, the book of Esther, Job, the Psalms of David, the Proverbs or Sentences of Solomon, the book of Ecclesiastes, called the Preacher, the Song of Solomon, also, the book of Isaiah, Jeremiah, Lamentations of Jeremiah, Ezekiel, Daniel, Hosea, Joel, Amos, Obadiah, Jonas, Micah, Nahum, Habakkuk, Zephaniah, Haggai Zachariah, Malachi. Also, the Holy Gospel according to St. Matthew, according to St. Mark, according to St. Luke, and according to St. John. Also, the second book of St. Luke, otherwise called the Acts of the Apostles. Also, the Epistles of St. Paul, to the Romans 1, to the Corinthians 2, to the Galatians 1, to the Ephesians 1, to the Philippians 1, to the Colossians 1, to the Thessalonians 2, to Timothy 2, to Titus 1, to Philemon 1. Also, the Epistle to the Hebrews, the Epistle of St. James, the first and second Epistle of St. Peter, the first, second and third Epistle of St. John, the Epistle of St. Jude. Also, the Apocalypse or Revelation of St. John.

IV.—Nous connoisons ces livres être Canoniques, et la règle très certaine de notre Foi: non tant par le commun accord et consentement de l'Eglise, que par le témoignage et persuasion intérieure du S. Esprit, qui nous les fait discerner d'avec les autres Ecclésiastiques, sur lesquels, encore qu'il soient utiles, on ne peut fonder aucun Article de Foi.

IV.—We know these books to be canonical, and the sure rule of our faith, not so much by the common agreement and consent of the Church, as by the internal testimony and persuasion of the Holy Spirit, who enables us to distinguish them from the other ecclesiastical books, upon which, although they may be useful, we cannot found any article of faith.

V.—Nous croyons que la Parole qui est continue en ces livres, est procedée de Dieu, duquel seul elle prend son autorité, et non des hommes. Et d'autant qu'elle est la règle de toute verité, contenant tout ce qui est nècessaire pour le service de Dieu et de notre salut, il n'est pas loisible aux hommes, ni même aux Anges, d'y ajouter, diminuer ou changer. D'où il s'ensuit que ni antiquité, ni les coûtumes, ni la multitude, ni la sagesse humaine, ni les jugemens, ni les arrêts, ni les édits, ni les decrets, ni les conciles, ni les visions, ni les miracles, ne doivent être opposez à cette Ecriture Sainte ; mais au contraire, toutes choses doivent être examinées, réglées, et reformées selon elle. Et suivant cela nous avoüons les trois Symboles, savior des Apôtres, de Nicée, et d'Athanese, parce qu'ils sont conformes à la Parole de Dieu.

V.—We believe that the word, which is contained in these books, proceeded from God, from whom only it derives its authority, and not from men: and forasmuch as it is the rule of all truth, containing all that is necessary for the service of God, and for our salvation, it is not lawful for men, nor even for angels, to add to it, diminish, or change it. Hence it follows, that neither antiquity, nor customs, nor the multitude, nor human wisdom, nor judgments, nor acts, nor edicts, nor decrees, nor councils, nor visions, nor miracles, ought to be opposed to these Holy Scriptures ; but, on the contrary, all things ought to be examined, ordered and reformed, according to them: and we do therefore acknowledge the three creeds, namely, of the Apostles, of Nice, and of Athanasius, because they are conformable to the word of God.

VI.—Cette Ecriture Sainte nous enseigne qu'en cette seule et simple essence Divine, que nous avons confessée, il y a trois personnes, le Père, le Fils, et le S. Esprit. Le Père, premiere cause, principe et origine de toutes choses. Le Fils, sa Parole et Sapience éternelle. Le S. Esprit, sa vertu, puissance et efficace. Le Fils, éternellement engendré du Père. Le. S. Esprit, procedant éternellement de tous deux : les trois personnes non confuses, mais distinctes, et toutefois non divisées, mais d'une même essence, éternité, puissance et égalité. Et en cela avoüons ce qui a été determiné par les Conciles Anciens, et détestons toutes sectes et hérésies qui ont été rejettées par les Saints Docteurs, comme S.

VI.—These Holy Scriptures teach us, that in this single and simple divine essence which we have confessed, there are three persons, the Father, the Son, and the Holy Spirit. The Father, the first cause, the principle, and the origin of all things ; the Son, his word and eternal wisdom ; the Holy Spirit, his virtue, power and efficacy. The Son eternally begotten of the Father ; the Holy Spirit proceeding from both ; the three persons not confounded, but distinct, and nevertheless not divided, but of the same essence, eternity, power, and equality. And in this we acknowledge what was determined by the ancient councils, and we detest all sects and heresies, which are rejected by the Holy Doctors,

Hilaire, S. Athanase, S. Ambroise, et S. Cyrille.

VII.—Nous croyons que Dieu en trois personnes co-operantes, par sa vertu sagesse et bonté incompréhensible, a crée toutes choses, non seulement le Ciel, la Terre et tout ce qui y est contenu ; mais aussi les esprits invisibles, desquels les uns sont déchus et trébuchez en perdition, les autres ont pérsisté en obeissance. Que les premiers s'étant corrompus en malice, sont ennemis de tout bien, par conséquent de toute l'Eglise. Les seconds ayant été prêservez par la grace de Dieu sont Ministres pour glorifier le nom de Dieu, et servir au salut de ses élus.

VIII.—Nous croyons que non seulement il a créé toutes choses, mais qu'il les gouverne et conduit, disposant, ordonnant selon sa volonté de tout ce qui avient au Monde : non pas qu'il soit auteur du mal, ou que la coulpe lui en puisse être imputée, vû que sa volonté est la règle souveraine et infaillible de toute droiture et équité : mais il a des moyens admirables de se servir tellement des diables et des mèchans, qu'il sait convertir en bien le mal qu'il font, et duquel ils sont coupables. Et ainsi, en confessant que rien ne se fait sans la providence de Dieu, nous adorons en humilité les secrets qui nous sont cachez, sans nous enquirer par-dessus notre mesure : mais plutôt appliquons à notre usage ce qui nous est montré en l'Ecriture Sainte pour être en repos et sureté, d'autant que Dieu, qui a toutes choses sujettes à soi, veille sur nous d'un

such as St. Hilary, St. Athanasius, St. Ambrose, and St. Cyril.

VII.—We believe that God, in three cöoperating persons, by his incomprehensible power, wisdom and goodness, created all things, not only the heavens, the earth, and all that in them is, but also the invisible spirits, of whom some are fallen and sunk into perdition, others have remained steadfast in obedience: that the first, being corrupt through malice, are enemies of all good, consequently of the whole Church; that the second, having been preserved by the grace of God, are ministers to glorify the name of God, and to aid in the salvation of his elect.

VIII.—We believe that he not only created all things, but that he governs and directs them, disposing and ordering according to his will every thing which comes to pass in the world : not that he is the author of evil, or that sin can thence be imputed to him, seeing that his will is the supreme and unerring rule of all right and equity; but that he possesses wonderful means of so availing himself of the devils and of the wicked, that he knows how to convert into good the evil which they do, and of which they are guilty. And thus, in confessing that nothing comes to pass without the providence of God, we humbly adore the secrets, which are hidden from us, without inquiring beyond our capacity; but rather let us apply to our use that which is set forth in the Holy Scriptures for our peace and safety, since God, who has all things subject to

soin paternel, tellement qu'il ne tombera point un cheveu de notre tête sans sa volonté. Et cependant il tient les diables et tous nos ennemis bridez, en sorte qu'ils ne nous peuvent faire aucune nuisance sans son congé.

IX.—Nous croyons que l'homme ayant éte créé pur et entier, et conforme à l'image de Dieu, est par sa propre faute dèchu de la grace qu'il avoit reçuë. Et ainsi s'est aliéné de Dieu, qui est la fontaine de justice et de tous biens, en sorte que sa nature est du tout corrompuë. Et étant aveuglé en son esprit, et dépravé en son cœur, a perdu toute intégrité sans avoir rien de reste. Et bien qu'il ait encore quelque discretion du bien et du mal, nonobstant nous disons, que ce qu'il a de clarté, se convertit en tenèbres, quand il est question de chercher Dieu: tellement qu'il n'en peut nullement approcher par son intelligence et raison. Et bien qu'il ait une volonté par laquelle il est incité à faire ceci ou cela: toutefois elle est du tout captive sous péché en sorte qu'il n'a nulle liberté à bien, que celle que Dieu lui donne.

X.—Nous croyons que toute la lignée d'Adam est infectée de telle contagion, qui est le péché originel, et un vice héréditaire, et non pas seulement une imitation, comme les Pelagiens ont voulu dire, lesquels nous détestons en leurs erreurs. Et n'estimons pas qu'il soit besoin de s'enquérir comme le péché vient d'un homme à l'autre, vû qûe c'est assez, que ce que Dieu lui avoit donné n'étoit pas pour lui seul, mais pour toute sa lignée: et

him, watches over us with paternal care, so that not a hair shall fall from our heads without his will. And in the meanwhile he restrains the devils and all our enemies, so that they can do us no harm except by his permission.

IX.—We believe that man, having been created pure and perfect, and in the image of God, has by his own fault fallen from the grace which he had received, and has thus alienated himself from God, who is the fountain of righteousness and of all good, so that his nature is altogether corrupt, and being blinded in his understanding and depraved in his heart, has lost all innocence, having nothing left. And although he still has some discernment of good and evil, nevertheless we say that light is turned into darkness, when he desires to seek God, so that he can by no means draw nigh unto him by his own intelligence and reason. And although he has a will, by which he is moved to do this or that, this will is nevertheless subject to sin, so that he is not free to do good, except so far as God enables him.

X.—We believe that the whole race of Adam is infected with the like contagion, which is *Original Sin*, and a hereditary defect, and not merely an imitation, as the Pelagians would say, whom we detest in their errors. And let us not deem it necessary to inquire how sin passeth from one man to another, seeing it sufficeth, that what God had given him was not for himself only, but for all his race, and thus that in his person

ainsi, qu'en la personne d'icelui nous avons été dénuez de tous biens, et sommes trébuchez en toute pauvreté et malediction.

we have been divested of all good, and are fallen into all poverty and condemnation.

XI.—Nous croyons aussi que ce vice est vraiment péché, qui suffit à condamner tout le genre humain, jusques aux petits enfans dès le ventre de la mere, et que pour tel il est reputé devant Dieu ; même qu'après le Baptême, c'est toûjours péché quant à la coulpe, bien que la condamnation en soit abolie aux enfans de Dieu, ne la leur imputant point par sa bonté gratuite. Outre cela, que c'est une perversité produisant toujours des fruits de malice et de rebellion, tels que les plus saints, encore qu'ils y resistent ne laissent point d'être entachez d'infirmitéz et de fautes, pendant qu'ils habitent en ce monde.

XI.—We believe also, that this defect is truly sin, which sufficeth to condemn the whole human race, even little children from the mother's womb, and that it is accounted such before God. That even after baptism, it is still sin as to its blame-worthiness, although condemnation therefor be abolished in the children of God, he not imputing it to them, through his free grace. Moreover, that it is a perversity, producing always such fruits of malice and rebellion, that the most holy, although they do resist it, cease not to be stained by infirmities and errors, whilst they sojourn in this world.

XII.—Nous croyons que de cette corruption et condamnation générale, en laquelle tous les hommes sont plongez, Dieu retire ceux, lesquels en son Conseil éternel et immuable, il a élus par sa seule bonté et misericorde en notre Seigneur Jesus-Christ sans considération de leurs œuvres, laissant des autres en cette même corruption et condamnation, pour démontrer en eux sa justice, comme aux premiers il fait luire les richesses de sa misericorde. Car les uns ne sont point meilleurs que les autres, jusques à ce que Dieu les discerne, selon son Conseil immuable, qu'il a déterminé en Jesus-Christ, devant la création du Monde: et nul aussi ne se pourroit introduire à un tel bien de sa propre vertu, vû que de notre nature nous ne pouvons avoir un seul bon mouvement, ni affection,

XII.—We believe that from this general corruption and condemnation, into which all men are plunged, God redeemeth those, whom by his eternal and immutable counsel, he hath elected, through his mere goodness and mercy, in our Lord Jesus Christ, without consideration of their works, leaving the rest in the same corruption and condemnation, to show forth in them his justice, as upon the first he causes to shine the riches of his mercy. For these are in no wise better than those, until God separates them according to his immutable counsel, which he determined in Jesus Christ, before the foundation of the world: And moreover, no one can attain unto such good of his own merits, seeing that by our nature we are incapable of a single good emotion,

ni pensée, jusques à ce que Dieu nous ait prévenus et nous y ait disposez.

affection, or thought, until God hath prepared and disposed us thereto.

XIII.—Nous croyons qu'en icelui Jesus-Christ tout ce qui étoit requis à notre salut nous a été offert et communiqué. Lequel nous étant donné à salut, nous a été quant et quant fait sapience, justice, sanctification et redemption: en sorte qu'en declinant de lui, on renonce à la misericorde du Père, ou il nous convient avoir refuge unique.

XIII.—We believe that through this same Jesus Christ, all that was necessary for our salvation has been offered and communicated to us. Who, being given to us for our salvation, has at the same time been made unto us wisdom, righteousness, sanctification and redemption: So that in falling away or withdrawing from him, we renounce the mercy of the Father, who should be our only refuge.

XIV.—Nous croyons que Jesus-Christ étant la sagesse de Dieu, et son Fils éternel, a vêtu notre chair, afin d'être Dieu et homme en une personne, même homme semblable à nous, passible en corps et en ame, sinon entant qu'il a été pur de toute macule. Et quant a son humanité, qu'il a été vraye semence d'Abraham et de David, bien qu'il ait été conçu par la vertu secrete du Sainte Esprit. En quoi, nous detestons toutes les hérésies, qui ont anciennement troublé les Eglises: et notamment aussi les imaginations diaboliques de Servet, lequel attribuë au Seigneur Jesus une divinité fantastique, d'autant qu'il le dit être idée et Patron de toutes choses, et le nomme Fils personnel ou figuratif de Dieu: Et finalement lui forge un corps de trois élémens incréez, ainsi mesle et détruit toutes les deux natures.

XIV.—We believe that Jesus Christ, being the wisdom ot God and his eternal Son, took upon him our flesh, to the end that he might be God and man in one person, very man, like unto us, liable to suffering in body and soul, only that he was pure and without spot. And as to his humanity, that he was the true seed of Abraham and David, although he was conceived by the secret power of the Holy Spirit. Herein we detest all the heresies which in former times troubled the churches, and especially also, the diabolical imaginations of Servetus, who attributes to the Lord Jesus a fantastic divinity, inasmuch as he says that he is the idea and pattern of all things, and calls him the personal or figurative Son of God, and finally devises for him a body composed of three uncreated elements, thus confounding and destroying the two natures.

XV.—Nous croyons qu'en une même personne assavoir Jesus-Christ, les deux natures sont vraiment et inséparablement conjointes

XV.—We believe that in one and the same person, namely, Jesus Christ, the two natures are truly and inseparably conjoined and

et unies, demeurant neanmoins chacune nature en sa proprieté distincte: tellement que comme en cette conjonction la nature Divine, retenant sa proprieté, est demeurée increé, infinie, et remplissant toutes choses: aussi la nature humaine est demeurée finie, ayant sa forme, mesure et proprieté, et même bien qué Jesus-Christ en ressuscitant ait donné l'immortalité à son corps, toutefois il ne lui a pas ôté la verité de sa nature. Et ainsi, nous le considerons tellement en sa divinité, que nous ne le depuillons point de son humanité.

XVI.—Nous croyons que Dieu envoyant son Fils, a voulu montrer son amour et bonté inestimable envers nous, en le livrant à la mort, et le ressuscitant pour accomplir toute justice, et pour nous acquerir la vie céleste.

XVII.—Nous croyons que par le sacrifice unique, que le Seigneur Jesus a offert en la croix, nous sommes reconciliez à Dieu, pour être tenus et reputez justes devant lui: parce que nous ne lui pouvons être agréables, ni être participans de son adoption, sinon d'autant qu'il nous pardonne nos fautes, et les ensevelit. Ainsi nous protestons que Jesus-Christ est notre lavement entier et parfait: qu'en sa mort nous avons entiere satisfaction pour nous acquitter de nos forfaits et iniquitez, dont nous sommes coupables, et ne pouvons être déliverez que par ce remede.

XVIII.—Nous croyons que toute notre justice est fondée en la remission de nos péchez, comme aussi c'est notre seule felicité, comme dit David. C'est pourquois

united, each nature preserving, however, its distinctive property: so that, as in this union, the Divine nature retaining its property, still continued uncreated, infinite, and filling all things, so the human nature still continued finite, having its form, measure and property, and even although Jesus Christ, in rising from the dead, hath given immortality to his body, nevertheless he hath not taken from it the reality of its nature: and thus we so consider him in his divinity, that we divest him not of his humanity.

XVI.—We believe that God, in sending his Son, was willing to manifest his inestimable love and goodness towards us, by delivering him up to death, and raising him again to fulfil all righteousness, and to obtain for us eternal life.

XVII.—We believe that by the one sacrifice, which the Lord Jesus offered upon the cross, we are reconciled to God, so as to be esteemed and accounted righteous before him, because we cannot be acceptable to him, nor be partakers of his adoption, except so far as he pardons our faults and blots them out. Thus we declare that Jesus Christ is our entire and perfect purification, that in his death we have complete satisfaction, to acquit us of the trespasses and sins whereof we are guilty, and from which we can be delivered only by this means.

XVIII.—We believe that all our righteousness is founded on the remission of our sins, as it is also our only blessedness, as David said. Wherefore, we reject all

nous rejettons tous autres moyens ne nous pouvoir justifier devant Dieu ; et sans présumer de nulles vertus ni merites, nous tenons simplement à l'obeïssance de Jesus-Christ, laquelle nous est allouée, tant pour couvrir toutes nos fautes, que pour nous faire trouver grace et faveur devant Dieu. Et de fait, nous croyons qu'en declinant de ce fondement tant peu que ce soit, nous de pourrions trouver ailleurs aucun repos, mais serions toujours agitez d'inquietude : d'autant que jamais nous ne sommes paisibles avec Dieu, jusques à ce que nous soyions bien resolus d'être aimez en Jesus-Christ, vû que nous sommes dignes d'être haïs en nous mêmes.

other means of being able to justify ourselves before God, and without presuming on any virtue or merit of our own, we rely simply on the obedience of Jesus Christ, which is imputed to us as well to cover all our faults, as to enable us to find grace and favour before God. And, indeed, we believe that in falling away from this foundation, ever so little, we could find no comfort elsewhere, but should be always disquieted : so that we never are at peace with God, until we are fully resolved to be loved in Jesus Christ, seeing that in ourselves we deserve to be hated.

XIX.—Nous croyons que c'est par ce moyen, que nous avons liberté et privilége d'invoquer Dieu, avec pleine fiance qu'il ce montrera notre Père. Car nous n'aurions aucun accès au Père, si nous n'étions addressez par ce Médiateur. Et pour être exaucez en son Nom, il convient tenir notre vie de lui comme de notre chef.

XIX.—We believe that we have by this means, the liberty and privilege of calling upon God, with full confidence that he will manifest himself our Father. For we should have no access to the Father, save through this Mediator. And that to be heard in his name, we must hold our life of him, as our head.

XX.—Nous croyons que nous sommes faits participans de cette justice par la seule fois : comme il est dit, qu'il a souffert pour nous acquerir le salut, afin que quiconque croira en lui, ne périsse point. Et que cela ce fait, d'autant que les promesses de vie, que nous sont données en lui, sont appropriées à notre usage, et en sentons l'effet, quand nous les acceptons, ne doutant point qu'étant assurez par la bouche de Dieu, nous ne serons point frustrez. Ainsi la justice que nous obtenons par la foi dé-

XX.—We believe that we are made partakers of this righteousness by faith only, as it is said, he suffered to purchase salvation for us, to the end that whosoever believeth in him shall not perish, and that this doth come to pass, inasmuch as the promises of life which are given to us in him, are appropriated to our use, and we feel their influence, when we accept them, nothing doubting, but that being assured by the mouth of God, we shall not be frustrated. Thus the righteousness which we obtain

pend des promesses gratuites, par lesquelles Dieu nous déclare et testifie qu'il nous aime.

through faith, depends on the gracious promises by which God declares and testifies to us that he loves us.

XXI.—Nous croyons que nous sommes illuminez en la foi par la grace secrete du Sainte Esprit, tellement que c'est un don gratuit et particulier que Dieu départ à ceux que bon lui semble, en sorte que les fidèles n'ont dequoi s'en glorifier, étant obligez au double, de ce qu'ils ont été preferez aux autrez. Même que la foi n'est pas seulement baillée pour un coup aux élus pour les introduire au bon chemin, mais pour les y faire continuer aussi jusques au bout. Car comme c'est à Dieu de faire le commencement, aussi c'est à lui de parachever.

XXI.—We believe that we are enlightened in faith, by the secret grace of the Holy Spirit, so that it is a free and special gift which God imparts to whomsoever he pleaseth, so that the faithful have nothing wherein to glory, being under a twofold obligation, forasmuch as they have been preferred to others. Moreover, that faith is not vouchsafed to the elect, only for a time, to lead them into the right way, but also to enable them to continue therein, even unto the end. For as it is with God to begin, so likewise is it for him to finish.

XXII.—Nous croyons que par cette foi nous sommes régénérez en nouveauté de vie, étant naturellement asservis à péché. Or nous recevons par foi la grace de vivre saintement, et en la crainte de Dieu, en recevant la promesse qui nous est donnée par l'Evangile, savoir que Dieu nous donnera son S. Esprit. Ainsi la foi non seulement ne refroidit pas l'affection de bien et saintement vivre, mais l'engendre et excite en nous, produisant necessairement les bonnes œuvres. Au reste, bien que Dieu, pour accomplir notre salut, nous régénére, nous reformant à bien faire, toutefois nous confessons que les bonnes œuvres, que nous faisons par la conduite de son Esprit, ne viennent point en compte pour nous justifier, ou mériter que Dieu nous tienne pour ses enfans, parce que nous serions toujours flottans en doute

XXII.—We believe that through this faith we are regenerate in newness of life, being naturally under bondage to sin, but now we receive by faith, the grace to live in holiness, and in the fear of God, on receiving the promise which is given to us by the Gospel, namely, that God will give us his Holy Spirit. Thus faith not only does not lessen the desire to live well and holily, but begets and excites it in us, producing necessarily good works: finally, although God, in order to bring about our salvation, regenerates us, fashioning us anew unto well doing, nevertheless we confess that the good works which we do under the guidance of his Spirit are accounted nothing in justifying us, or in rendering us worthy to be esteemed the children of God, because we should be always wavering in doubt and disquiet,

et inquietude, si nos consciences ne s'appuyoient sur la satisfaction par laquelle Jesus-Christ nous a acquittez.

XXIII.—Nous croyons que toutes les figures de la Loi ont pris fin à la venuë de Jesus-Christ. Mais bien que les cérémonies ne soient plus en usage, neanmoins la substance et vérité nous en est demeurée en la personne de celui auquel git tout accomplissement. Au surplus, il nous fait aider de la Loi et des Prophétes, tant pour regler notre vie, que pour être confirmez aux promesses de l'Evangile.

XXIV.—Nous croyons, puis que Jesus-Christ nous est donné pour seul Avocat, et qu'il nous commande de nous retirer privément en son Nom vers son Père: et même qu'il ne nous est pas licite de prier sinon en suivant la forme que Dieu nous a dictée par sa Parole: que tout ce que les hommes ont imaginée de l'intercession des Saints trépassez, n'est qu'abus et fallace de Satan, pour faire dévoyer les hommes de la forme de bien prier. Nous rejettons aussi tous autres moyens que les hommes présument avoir pour se racheter envers Dieu, comme dérogeans, au sacrifice de la mort et passion de Jesus-Christ. Finalement nous tenons le Purgatoire pour une illusion procedée de cette même boutique, de laquelle sont aussi procedez les vœux monastiques, pélérinages, défense du mariage, et de l'usuage des viandes, l'observation cérémonielle des jours, la Confession Auriculaire, les Indulgences, et toutes autres telles choses, par lesquelles

if our consciences did not rest upon the satisfaction by which Jesus Christ has acquitted us.

XXIII.—We believe that all the types of the law were fulfilled at the coming of Jesus Christ; but although its ceremonies are no longer in use, nevertheless their substance and truth have remained to us in the person of him in whom all things were accomplished. Moreover, we must seek for help from the law and the prophets, as well to regulate our lives as to be confirmed in the promises of the Gospel.

XXIV.—We believe, since Jesus Christ is given to us as our only advocate, and since he commands us to draw nigh unto his Father secretly in his name. and since it is not even lawful for us to pray, save as God hath enjoined on us by his word, that all which men have imagined of the intercession of departed saints is only abuse and deceitfulness of Satan, to lead men astray from the form of sound words in prayer. We reject, also, all other means which men presume to employ for their ransom with God, as undervaluing the sacrifice of the death and passion of Jesus Christ. Finally, we hold purgatory to be an illusion proceeding from the same source, whence have also proceeded monastic vows, pilgrimages, prohibitions of marriage and of the use of meats, the ceremonial observance of days, auricular confession, indulgences, and all such other things, through which they think to deserve grace and salvation. Which things we reject, not only

on pense mériter grace et salut. Lesquelles choses nous rejettons, non seulement pour la fausse opinion du mérite qui y est attaché, mais assui parce que ce sont inventions humaines qui imposent joug aux consciences.

XXV.—Or, parce que nous ne jouïssons de Jesus-Christ que par l'Evangile, nous croyons que l'ordre de l'Eglise, qui a été établi en son autorité, doit être sacré et inviolable, et partant que l'Eglise ne peut subsister sinon qu'il y ait des Pasteurs qui ayent la charge d'enseigner, lesquels on doit honorer et écouter en révérence quand ils sont duëment appellez, et exercent fidellement leur office. Non pas que Dieu soit attaché à telles aides ou moyens inferieurs: mais parce qu'il lui plait nous entretenir sous telle bride. En quois nous détestons tous fantastiques, qui voudroient bien, entant qu'en eux est, anéantir le ministere et prédication de la parole de Dieu et des sacremens.

XXVI.—Nous croyons donc que nul ne se doit retirer à part, et se contenter de sa personne: mais que tous ensembles doivent garder et entretenir l'union de l'Eglise, se soumettant à l'instruction commune, et au joug Jesus-Christ: et ce en quelque lieu où Dieu aura établi un vrai ordre de l'Eglise, encore que les Magistrates et leurs édits y soient contraires, que tous ceux qui ne s'y rangent, ou s'en séparent, contrarient à l'ordonnance de Dieu.

XXVII.—Toutefois nous croyons qu'il convient discerner soigneuse-

on account of the false opinion of the merit which is attached to them, but also because they are human inventions, which impose a yoke on the conscience.

XXV.—Now, because we enjoy Jesus Christ only through the Gospel, we believe that the order of the Church, which has been established under his authority, ought to be sacred and inviolate, and forasmuch as the Church cannot subsist unless there are pastors who have the charge of teaching, whom we ought to honour and hearken to with reverence, when they are duly called and faithfully exercise their office. Not that God is held to the use of such aids or inferior means, but because it pleaseth him to keep us under such restraint: in which respect we detest all visionaries, who would, as far as in them lies, destroy the ministry, and the preaching of the Word of God, and of the sacraments.

XXVI.—We believe, then, that no one ought to withdraw himself, and be satisfied with himself alone, but that all should together watch over and preserve the union of the Church, submitting to common instruction and to the yoke of Jesus Christ, and this, wherever God shall have established a true order of the Church, although magistrates and their edicts are contrary thereto, and that all who do not place themselves under it, or who separate themselves from it, resist the ordinance of God.

XXVII.—Nevertheless we believe that it is meet to distinguish

ment, et avec prudence, qu'elle est la vraye Eglise: parce que par trop on abuse de ce titre. Nous disons donc, suivant la Parole de Dieu, que c'est la compagnie des fideles, qui s'accordent à suivre cette Parole, et la pure Religion qui en dépend, et qui profitent en elle tout le tems de leur vie, croissant et se confirmant en la crainte de Dieu, selon qu'ils ont besoin de s'avancer et de marcher toujours plus outre. Même quoi qu'ils s'efforcent, qu'il leur convient avoir incessament recourse à la remission de leurs péchez, néanmoins nous ne nions point que parmi les fideles il n'y ait des hypocrites et reprouvez, desquels la malice ne peut effacer le titre de l'Eglise.

XXVIII.—Sous cette créance nous protestons que la où la parole de Dieu n'est point recuë, et où on ne fait nulle profession de s'assujettir à elle, et où il n'y a nul usage des Sacremens: à parler proprement, on ne peut juger qu'il y ait aucune Eglise. Partant nous condamnons les assemblées de la Papauté, vû que la pure vérité de Dieu en est bannie, esquelles les Sacremens sont corrompus, abâtardis, falsifiez, ou anéantis du tout: et esquelles toutes superstitions et idolatries ont la vogue. Nous tenons donc que tout ceux qui se mêlent en tels actes, et y communiquent, se séparent et retranchent du Corps de Jesus-Christ. Toutefois, parce qu'il reste encore quelque petite trace d'Eglise en la Papauté, et même que la vertu et substance du Batême y est demeurée, joint que l'efficace du Batême ne dépend pas de celui qui l'administre: nous

carefully and prudently which is the true Church. because this title is too much abused. We say then, according to the word of God, that it is the company of the faithful, who agree to follow this word and the pure religion which depends upon it, and who profit by it all the days of their lives, growing and strengthening themselves in the fear of God, according as they have need of improvement, and of still proceeding onwards. Indeed, howsoever they may strive, they must constantly rely on the remission of their sins, nevertheless we do not deny that there are among the faithful some hypocrites and reprobates, whose malice cannot destroy the title of the Church.

XXVIII.—Under this belief, we protest, that where the word of God is not received, and where subjection to it is not professed, and where no use is made of the sacraments, there, properly speaking, we cannot think there is any Church ; wherefore we condemn the assemblies of the papacy, seeing that the pure truth of God is banished from them, in which the sacraments are corrupted, debased, falsified, or altogether destroyed, and in which all superstitions and idolatry prevail. We hold, then, that all who take part in such acts, and communicate therein, separate and cut themselves off from the body of Jesus Christ. Nevertheless, as there still remaineth some slight trace of the Church in papacy, and as even the virtue and the substance of baptism hath continued therein, besides which the efficacy of baptism doth not depend upon him who administers it,

confessions ceux qui y sont baptisez n'avoir besoin d'un second Batême. Cependant à cause des corruptions qui y sont, on n'y peut présenter les enfans sans se polluer.

we confess that those who are baptized therein have no need of a second baptism. However, by reason of the corruptions which exist therein, we cannot present our children there without polluting ourselves.

XXIX.—Quant est de la vraye Eglise, nous croyons qu'elle doit être gouvernée selon la Police que notre Seigneur Jesus-Christ a établie: C'est qu'il y ait des Pasteurs, des Surveillans et des Diacres, afin que la pure doctrine ait son cours, que les vices soient corrigez et reprimez, et que les pauvres et tous autres affligez soient secourus en leurs necessitez: et que les assemblées se fassent au nom de Dieu, esquelles grands et petits soient édifiez.

XXIX.—With regard to the true Church, we believe that it ought to be governed according to the polity which our Lord Jesus Christ hath established. That is to say. that there are Pastors, Overseers and Deacons, to the end that pure doctrine may have its course, that vice may be corrected and repressed, and that the poor, and all others in affliction, may be relieved, according to their necessities, and that assemblies may be held in the name of God, in which high and low may be edified.

XXX.—Nous croyons tous vrais Pasteurs, en quel que lieu qu'ils soient, avoir même autorité et egale puissance sous un seul chef, seul souverain, et seul universel Evêque, Jesus-Christ: et pour cette cause, que nulle Eglise ne doit prétendre aucune domination ou Seigneurie sur l'autre.

XXX.—We believe that all true Pastors, in whatever place they may be, have the same authority, and equal power, under one sole chief, sole sovereign, and sole universal Bishop, Jesus Christ, and therefore, for this reason, no Church ought to claim any dominion or sovereignty over another.

XXXI.—Nous croyons que nul ne se doit ingerer de son autorité propre pour gouverner l'Eglise: mais que cela se doit faire par élection, etant qu'il est possible et que Dieu le permet. Laquelle exception nous y ajoutons notamment, parce qu'il a falu quelquefois, et même de notre tems, (auquel l'état de l'Èglise étoit interrompu,) que Dieu ait suscité des gens d'une facon extraordinaire, pour dresser l'Eglise de nouveau, qui étoit en ruine et

XXXI.—We believe that no one ought, of his own authority, to take upon himself to govern the Church, but that this should be done by election, as far as possible, and God permitting. Which exception we do especially make, because it hath been necessary, and even in our time, (when the order of the Church was interrupted,) that God should raise up persons, by extraordinary means, to build anew the Church, which lay in ruin and desolation. But be

désolation. Mais quoiqu'il en soit, nous croyons qu'il se faut toujours conformer à cette regle, que tous Pasteurs, Surveillans et Diacres ayent témoignage d'être appellez â leur office.

XXXII. — Nous croyons aussi qu'il est bon et utile, que ceux qui sont élus pour être Superintendans, avisent entr'eux quel moyen ils devront tenir pour le régime de tout le corps, et toutefois qu'ils ne déclinent nullement de ce qui nous en a été donné par notre Seigneur Jesus-Christ. Ce qui n'empêche point qu'il n'y ait qu'elques Ordonnances particulieres en chacun lieu, selon que la commodite le requerra.

XXXIII.—Cependant nous excluons toutes inventions humaines, et toutes Loiz qu'on voudroit introduire sous ombre du service de Dieu, par lesquelles on voudroit lier les consciences: mais seulement recevons ce qui fait et est propre pour nourrir la concorde, et tenir chacun depuis le premier jusqu'au dernier en obeïssance. En quoi nous avons à suivre ce que notre Seigneur Jesus a déclaré quant à l'excommunication: laquelle nous approuvons et confessons être nécessaire avec toutes ses appartenances.

XXXIV.—Nous croyons que les Sacremens sont ajoutez à la Parole pour plus ample confirmation, afin de nous être gages et marreaux de la grace de Dieu, et par ce moyen aider et soulager notre foi, à cause de l'infirmité et rudesse qui est en nous : et qu'ils sont tellement signes exterieurs, que Dieu opere par eux en la vertu de son Esprit,

this as it may, we believe that we must always conform to this rule, that all Pastors, Overseers and Deacons must have testimony of being called to their office.

XXXII.—We believe also, that it is good and useful, that those who are elected to be superintendents should consult together what means they ought to adopt for the government of the whole body, and nevertheless that they must in no wise depart from that which hath been ordained for us by our Lord Jesus Christ; which doth not hinder that there may be some particular ordinances in every place, as convenience may require.

XXXIII.—We exclude, however, all human inventions, and all laws that men would introduce under pretext of serving God, whereby they desire to fetter the conscience ; but we receive only what produces and is proper to nourish concord, and preserve every one from first to last in obedience. Wherein we are to follow what our Lord Jesus has declared concerning excommunication, which we approve and confess to be necessary, with all its appurtenances.

XXXIV.—We believe that the sacraments are added to the word for more ample confirmation, to be unto us pledges and tokens of the grace of God, and thus to assist and cherish our faith, because of our infirmities and imperfections, and that they are in such wise outward signs, that God works through them by the virtue of his

afin de nous y rien signifier en vain, toutefois nous tenons que toute leur substance et vérité est en Jesus-Christ: et si on les separe, ce n'est plus rien qu'ombrage et fumée.

Spirit, so as therein to set forth to us nothing in vain; nevertheless we hold that their substance and their truth are in Jesus Christ; and if we separate them, there remaineth nothing but shadow and vapour.

XXXV.—Nous en confessons seulement deux, communs à toute l'Eglise, desquels le premier, qui est le Batême, nous est donné pour témoignage de notre adoption: parce que là nous sommes entrez au Corps de Christ, afin d'être lavez et nettoyez par son Sang, et puis renouvellez en sainteté de vie par son Saint Esprit. Nous tenons aussi, bien que nous ne soyions baptisez qu'une fois, que le profit qui nous est la signifié s'étend à la vie et à la mort, afin que nous ayions une signature permanente, que Jesus-Christ nous sera toujours justice et sanctification. Or bien que ce soit un Sacrement de Foi et de Pénitence, neanmoins parce que Dieu reçoit en son Eglise les petits enfans avec leurs Pères, nous disons que par l'autorité de Jesus-Christ les petits enfans engendrez des fidelles doivent être baptisez.

XXXV.—We confess but two sacraments common to the whole Church, of which the first, which is baptism, is given to us in testimony of our adoption, because thereby we are grafted into the body of Christ, to the end that we might be washed and cleansed by his blood, and then be renewed in holiness of life by his Holy Spirit. We hold likewise, although we are baptized but once, that the benefit thereby signified to us extends to life and death, to the end that we may have an enduring testimony that Jesus Christ will always be to us righteousness and sanctification. Besides, although it is a sacrament of faith and of repentance, nevertheless, forasmuch as God doth receive into his Church little children with their fathers, we say, that by the authority of Jesus Christ, little children, begotten of the faithful, ought to be baptized.

XXXVI.—Nous confessons que la sainte Cene (qui est le second Sacrement) nous est un témoignage de l'union que nous avons avec Jesus-Christ: d'autant qu'il n'est pas seulement une fois mort et ressuscité pour nous, mais aussi nous repait et nourrit vraiment de sa chair et de son Sang à ce que nous soyions un avec lui: et que sa vie nous soit commune. Or bien qu'il soit au Ciel jusques à ce qu'il vienne pour juger tout le monde, toutefois nous croyons que

XXXVI.—We confess that the holy supper (which is the second sacrament) is to us a testimonial of our union with Jesus Christ: forasmuch as he not only once died and rose again for us, but also feeds and nourishes us truly with his flesh and his blood, in order that we may be one with him, and his life be common to us. Now, although he is in heaven until he shall come to judge the whole world, nevertheless we believe that by the secret and incompre-

par la vertu secrete et incompréhensible de son Esprit, il nous nourrit et vivifie de la substance de son Corps et de son Sang. Nous tenons bien que cela se fait spirituellement, non pas pour mettre au lieu de l'effet et de la vérité, imagination ni pensée: mais d'autant que ce mystère surmonte en sa hautesse la mesure de notre sens, et tout ordre de nature. Bref, parce qu'il est céleste, il ne peut être apprehendé que par Foi.

XXXVII.—Nous croyons (ainsi qu'il à été dit) que tant en la Cene qu'au Batême, Dieu nous donne rëellement et par effet ce qu'il y figure. Et partent nous joignons avec les signes la vraye possession et jouïssance de ce qui nous est là présenté. Et ainsi, tous ceux qui apportent à la table sacré de Christ une pure foi comme un vaisseau, reçoivent vraiment ce que les signes y testifient: c'est que le Corps et le Sang de Jesus-Christ ne servént pas moins de manger et de boire à l'ame, que le Pain et le Vin font au Corps.

XXXVIII.—Ainsi nous tenons que l'eau étant un élement caduque, ne laisse pas de nous testifier en vérité le lavement intérieur de notre ame au Sang de Jesus-Christ, par l'efficace de son Esprit, et que le Pain et le Vin nous étant donnez en là Cene nous servent vraiment de nourriture spirituelle, d'autant qu'ils nous montrent comme à l'œil, la chair de Jesus-Christ nous être notre viande, et son Sang notre breuvage. Et rejettons les les Fantastiques et Sacrémentaires, qui ne veulent récevoir tels signes et marques ; vû que notre Seign-

hensible virtue of his Spirit, he nourishes and quickens us with the substance of his body and of his blood. We do, however, hold that this is done spiritually, nor do we admit either imagination or opinion, as effect and truth, but forasmuch as this mystery surpasses in its height the measure of our understanding and the whole order of nature, in short, because it is heavenly, it cannot be apprehended but through faith.

XXXVII.—We believe (as it hath been said) that, as well in the supper as in the baptism, God gives us really and effectually what he therein figures to us, and therefore we connect with the symbols the true possession and enjoyment of what is there presented to us. And thus all who bring to the holy table of Christ a pure faith, as a vessel, receive truly what the symbols bear witness to, that is, that the body and the blood of Jesus Christ serve not less as meat and drink for the soul, than the bread and wine for the body.

XXXVIII.—Thus we hold that water, being a perishable element, nevertheless sufficeth to witness to us in truth, the inward washing of our souls by the blood of Jesus Christ, through the efficacy of his Spirit, and that bread and wine, being given to us in the supper, truly are to us spiritual nourishment, forasmuch as they present to us, as to the eye, the flesh of Jesus Christ as our meat, and his blood as our drink. And we reject those visionaries and sacramentarians, who will not receive such symbols and tokens, seeing that

eur Jesus prononce, ceci est mon Corps, et cette Coupe est mon Sang.

XXXIX. — Nous croyons que Dieu veut que le monde soit gouverné par Loix et Police, afin qu'il y ait quelque bride pour reprimer les appetits desordonnez du monde. Et ainsi, qu'il a établi les Royaumes, Republiques, et toutes autres sortes de Principautez, soit héréditaires ou autrement, et tout ce qui appartient à l'état de justice, et en veut être reconnu Auteur: à cette cause il a mis le glaive en la main des Magistrats pour reprimer les péchez commis non seulement contre la seconde Table des Commandemens de Dieu, mais aussi contre la premiere. Il faut donc à cause de lui, que non seulement on endure que les Supérieurs dominent, mais aussi qu'on les honore et prise en toute reverence, les tenans pour ses Lieutenans et Officiers, lesquels il a commis pour exercer une charge légitime et sainte.

XL.—Nous tenons donc qu'il faut obéïr à leurs Loix et Statuts, payer Tributs, Impôts, et autres devoirs, et porter le joug de subjection d'une bonne et franche volonté, encore qu'ils fussent infideles, moyennant que l'Empire souverain de Dieu demeure en son entier. Ainsi nous détestons ceux qui voudroient rejetter les Superioritez, mettre communauté et confusion de biens, et renverser l'ordre de la justice.

our Lord Jesus saith, this is my body, and this cup is my blood.

XXXIX.—We believe that God wills that the world should be governed by laws and polity, to the end that there may be some curb to restrain the disorderly appetites of mankind, and therefore that he hath established kingdoms, republics, and all other kinds of government, whether hereditary or otherwise, and all that appertaineth to justice, and requireth that he should be acknowledged their author: wherefore he hath committed the sword to the hand of the magistrate, to restrain transgressions, not only against the second table of the commandments of God, but also against the first. We must then, for his sake, not only submit to the authority of rulers, but also honour them and hold them in all reverence, accounting them as his vicegerents and officers, whom he hath appointed to fulfil a legitimate and holy charge.

XL.—We hold, then, that we must obey their laws and statutes, pay tribute, imposts and other duties, and bear the yoke of subjection freely and cheerfully, although they should be unbelievers, provided the sovereign empire of God remain entire: wherefore we detest those who would reject all authority, establish a community and a confusion of goods, and overturn the order of justice.

www.ingramcontent.com/pod-product-compliance
Lightning Source LLC
LaVergne TN
LVHW010255110826
845151LV00004B/1480
9781425522445